# COMPREHENSIVE

# SCHOOL

# GUIDANCE

# AND

# COUNSELING

# PROGRAM

# YOUR

# COMPREHENSIVE

# SCHOOL

# GUIDANCE

# AND

# COUNSELING

# PROGRAM

*a handbook of practical activities*

## c. e. vanzandt
**University of Southern Maine**

## j. b. hayslip
**Plymouth State College**

**Longman**
New York & London

**Your Comprehensive School Guidance and Counseling Program:
A Handbook of Practical Activities**

Longman, 10 Bank Street, White Plains, N.Y. 10606

Associated companies:
Longman Group Ltd., London
Longman Cheshire Pty., Melbourne
Longman Paul Pty., Auckland
Copp Clark Pitman, Toronto

Acquisitions editor: Stuart Miller
Production editor: Victoria Mifsud
Cover design and illustration: Kevin C. Kall
Text art: Fine Line, Inc.
Production supervisor: Anne Armeny

**Library of Congress Cataloging-in-Publication Data**

VanZandt, C. E.
    Your comprehensive school guidance and counseling program : a
handbook of practical activities / C. E. VanZandt and J. B. Hayslip.
        p.   cm.
    Includes bibliographical references (p.   ) and index.
    ISBN 0-8013-1147-0
    1. Educational counseling—Handbooks, manuals, etc.  I. Hayslip,
J. B. (Josephine B.)  II. Title.
LB1027.5.V296   1994
371.4—dc20                                          93-25770
                                                       CIP

1 2 3 4 5 6 7 8 9 10-ARM-9897969594

# Contents

# Preface

We, the co-authors, have worked together on a number of projects since 1975. We have written this handbook because we have both felt a need for functional training material for school counselors. We each teach a counselor education course—"Organization of School Guidance and Counseling Programs"—in our respective colleges. We have tried a number of textbooks over the years and have found them to be wonderful theoretical models, but our students, who are about to move into school guidance programs, need practical hands-on learning material.

We've organized this handbook as a process-oriented opportunity for the counselor education student to learn by application. Activities are provided to allow the student to practice guidance functions in the relatively safe environment of the college classroom. Students can play the roles of counselor, student, parent, or administrator. The handbook is based on a logical developmental approach. When students have completed it and the course, they will be prepared to organize school guidance programs on a developmental, comprehensive basis.

The contents of this handbook have been reviewed by practicing counselors and dedicated graduate students. Through their good questions, useful ideas, objective feedback, and candid comments we have made several revisions and added a great deal of information to the handbook.

Because of the importance of linking theory to practice, we will continue to use our respective required texts. The names of these texts plus some recommended readings are listed in Appendix A.

The 1990s have been a turning point for renewed emphasis on first determining the needs of the students and then bringing together the resources to meet these needs. Throughout the handbook, students are asked to develop their own model for delivering a comprehensive guidance and counseling program to all the students in a given school. We will provide some models, such as the New Hampshire Comprehensive Guidance and Counseling Program and the Maine Comprehensive Guidance Program, but only after students have started to conceptualize their own model, so as to encourage creativity and fresh ideas.

Throughout this adventure we ask students to keep in mind the Human Factor. Sometimes school counselors become so involved in the guidance process they forget that it is *people* with whom they are working. We are people working with other people; as human beings we have only ourselves and our expertise to offer in helping others to grow to the fullest development possible. Counselors must lead their programs in a human-directed manner, with the aim of encouraging everyone in the system to become involved in delivering a comprehensive, developmental guidance and counseling program.

## ACKNOWLEDGMENTS

Writing this handbook has been fun! The two of us became more and more excited about the project as it continued to evolve and as we included more people in making the dream a reality. As with any venture of this type, so many people were helpful in bringing the project to fruition that we would like to acknowledge their contributions.

We appreciate the work of Isabel Myers and Katherine Briggs (and all of their protégés who kept refining the use of the Myers-Briggs Type Indicator). While working on this book we have recognized the complementary strengths of an Extroverted, Intuitive, Thinking, Judging (Jo) and an Extroverted, Sensing, Thinking, Perceptive (Zark) partnership and we used our knowledge of the Myers-Briggs typologies to assist us in seeing the Big Picture and its parts. We had to process our own process and in doing so, had a great time rediscovering how much we enjoy writing with each other.

Two very special people have accompanied us on our mission to spread the word about comprehensive school guidance and counseling programs. James V. Carr, Vocational Guidance Consultant, New Hampshire Department of Education, and Nancy Perry, Guidance Consultant, Maine Department of Education, have been leaders in the movement to change school counseling from reactive services to proactive programs. We appreciate their wisdom, experience, and friendship.

Jo's husband, Ellwyn, has provided steady support from the early stages of the project, and his creative contributions to the graphic layout and design of the handbook have helped in the conceptualization of the paradigm. Ellwyn has a long history of lending his artistic talents in support of counselors.

Zark's wife, Kitty, has not only been supportive of the many hours spent in creating this handbook but has also contributed several very important activities that work for her in her setting as a director of guidance. In several instances, she has tried out an activity in her "real world" of guidance and returned with valuable information.

We are most appreciative of the contributions of our students at Plymouth State College and the University of Southern Maine. They have participated in the experiment to move to a model of cooperative learning in the counselor education classroom, and they have provided both the challenge and the reinforcement that has shaped the final product. Their questions have been insightful; their suggestions have been incorporated at all levels because they make so much sense; their excitement about being counselors and their dedication to their training has been inspirational. We can't wait for all of them to be out there in the schools reshaping the vision and image of school counseling.

We would like to thank the following reviewers for their helpful comments and suggestions:

Eldon Ruff, Indiana University, South Bend
Norman Gysbers, University of Missouri
Stanley Baker, Pennsylvania State University
Adam Scrupski, Rutgers University
Eileen Matthay, Southern Connecticut State University
Thomas Harrington, Northeastern University

Certainly, we want to acknowledge the cumulative contributions of thousands of superintendents, principals, specialists, parents, counselors, community leaders, colleagues, and leaders in the professional organizations who have helped to mold our thinking and perspective over the years. But most of all, we want to thank the students in kindergarten through twelfth grade with whom we have worked—because after all these years, we still believe that school counseling is the most noble of professions, and the students are the reason the job is so exciting and rewarding. It is because of the students that we want to help create school counseling programs that are the pride of the school system. They deserve only the best.

## A FINAL INSTRUCTION/OBSERVATION

We have field tested this handbook in six "Organization of Guidance Programs" classes. We are aware that any work can be improved, and we look forward to your input after you have used the handbook for a semester. Please complete the text evaluation form on the final pages of the handbook and return it to us. Thank you for your participation.

# Introduction

## HOW TO USE THIS HANDBOOK

This handbook is designed to teach students about the practical aspects of managing a school guidance and counseling program. It is not filled with extensive theory and philosophy. It is concerned with promoting useful methods of helping counselors be more productive and accountable, and challenging counselors to continually refine their own delivery systems.

In importance and relevance to the needs of both counselors and clients, a handbook on the management of guidance and counseling programs is essential if the practicing counselor is to maximize resources and services so that theory and process can flourish. The interdependent nature of the various facets of the counseling profession requires that the counselor seriously address the demands of a well-managed program.

The handbook is based on multidimensional models of guidance and counseling program management. It presents students with a number of models and also gives them the opportunity to develop their own. Experience suggests that the school guidance and counseling programs with the best reputations are those with well-thought-out program designs complemented by competent staff and leaders. Although some programs focus on specific services to meet the needs of targeted populations, the outstanding programs see the Big Picture and meet the needs of all the students.

The ability to perceive, respond to, and manage the whole spectrum of counseling is what this handbook is all about. With a multidimensional approach to guidance and counseling program management as a framework, the handbook identifies and describes the components (little pictures) of the total management scheme (big picture), then brings the entire experience back into focus for the counselor to synthesize and put into practical use.

## AUDIENCE

This handbook is designed primarily for counselor education classes typically listed in college catalogues as "Organization and Administration of Guidance and Counseling Programs." The authors' investigation of counselor education programs reveals that many do not require, or in some cases, even offer the course. We believe that this material should be required of all counselor education students who plan to work within a public school setting, and we believe this handbook will complement any assigned text.

Guidance directors or counselor supervisors who are interested in re-structuring their school counseling programs to meet the needs of a changing world and to be up-to-date with current trends in the counseling field make up another target group for this handbook. Guidance directors receive little or no training in how to manage a school counseling program; this book addresses that concern by offering a site-based management model. Counselors working together as cooperative learning teams can create quality programs that break the mold of traditional school counseling services.

The handbook is not just for program directors and school counselors, however. Counselors in any setting must understand the goals and services of the total program in order to complement those services. Being good team players is essential if counselors are to help realize the total impact a program can have on its clientele. If counselors understand the purposes, complexity, and interrelatedness of all aspects of a school guidance and counseling program, they may become more accepting of the less-than-engaging functions of the position. Or they will learn to delegate some of these functions to those in positions to handle them more appropriately. These not-so-glamorous functions exist in all counseling settings, not just in school environments, so the management skills may be put to use wherever efficient and comprehensive counseling programs are sought.

Counselors in private practice, counselors who are the sole proprietors of a regional office, or elementary school counselors cannot escape the need for management skills even though they may not see themselves as directly part of "the team." In fact, these individuals may be the most needy, for they are responsible for *everything* that happens in their work setting. If they fail to see the Big Picture, and limit their involvement to certain administrative duties, who will be responsible for the total management of the program? A careful, objective look at the counseling profession suggests that we all need good management and leadership skills.

## FOCUS

We are living in an age of accountability. Counselors, like all other profession-als, must respond to the demand for accountability. This handbook offers school counselors and counselor supervisors a framework in which to (1) view the total functioning of the guidance and counseling program and (2) perceive the various roles and functions that must be integrated into the total program for the counseling services to be truly accountable.

The handbook will also foster skills and knowledge in the areas of program development and supervision of counseling programs. These competencies are not solely the domain of program directors and supervisors; they are areas in which all counseling practitioners must demonstrate both skills and positive attitudes if counseling programs are to make the best use of their resources. By making a conscious effort to integrate their individual preferences with all other functions of the counseling program, counselors can help to develop a well-rounded and well-synthesized program.

If counselors are to help students reach their total potential, they need to model how they reach their own maximum performance as counselors. This handbook is designed to empower counselors to create the most effective programs, to assemble the best available resources, and to demonstrate their feelings of worth as counselors. This is an ambitious endeavor, but we have faith that all counselors truly want to be the best that they can be. We also believe that if counselors are open to change, they can empower themselves. The strategies and resources provided here will enhance that empowerment.

## METHOD

Both authors believe in the power of cooperative learning. In recent years, schools have found that a depth and richness of learning results from students working cooperatively to develop products or procedures: Group members' strengths surface and express themselves; group pressure urges some members to new heights of performance while other members learn how to encourage, motivate, and assert themselves; written and verbal communication skills are enhanced; team building and risk taking can be fostered and nurtured; shared responsibility becomes an acceptable norm; and a more holistic perspective leads to results of higher quality.

Listening to lectures on rare occasions can be scintillating; however, we believe that learning by doing can be a more empowering experience. Therefore, this handbook is designed with cooperative learning in mind. Most activities in the book are designed for small groups and, since we believe that as much can be gained from the process itself as from the final product, a means of "processing" the group experience is included at the end of the book.

## REFLECTIONS PAGES

At the end of each chapter, we have placed a reflections page. Please use these pages to reflect on your work, personally and as a group. If you write down your thoughts and feelings as you progress through your tasks, you will be able to return to these pages as you begin to assemble your final process and product. Although you are not required to share the personal notes that you accumulate, you might find these of valuable assistance to your group.

# YOUR

## COMPREHENSIVE

## SCHOOL

## GUIDANCE

## AND

## COUNSELING

## PROGRAM

# CHAPTER 1

# Why Counselors Need to Take This Handbook Seriously

As counselor educators, one of our favorite questions to ask students is *Why?* There are thousands—maybe millions—of Why questions counselors might ask. We'll get to them later. For a moment, however, we want you to ponder the question of Why. We believe that Why is one of the most critical words in a counselor's vocabulary if used with conviction and skill, so we're going to tell you why you should be asking Why.

When you were a child, did you become frustrated if you asked a question like, "Why do I have to go to school?" and you got a reply such as "Just because. . ." or "Because it's good for you"? Did you vow then that when you were an adult and children asked you that kind of question, you would give them a much better answer?

## DEVELOPING A RATIONALE

An unfortunate phenomenon evolved for many of us as we became adults: We found ourselves repeating the behavior that was modeled for us long ago. Now, when people have the audacity to challenge us with questions like, "Why do we need more counselors?" we find ourselves at a loss to provide truly substantive responses that will make the questioners become wide-eyed and truly receptive to our arguments.

Through the 1960s and early 1970s, schools were rarely challenged about the need for counselors—at the high school level, at least. The United States and the former Soviet Union were waging a battle for superiority in space, and the National Defense Education Act (NDEA) had been established to make our schools more competitive. Many counselors' positions were created with the intent of getting more students interested in taking math and science courses. However, once the trend shifted toward school counselors in the elementary grades, skeptics surfaced. Many wondered why "therapists" were needed in the schools; others questioned why students should be prepared for college so early. Trying to educate the public to extend its perceptions of school counseling beyond scheduling or getting students into college has been one of the major challenges of the profession.

In the 1970s and 1980s, *accountability* became more of a buzzword. Some counselors, however, especially those who had been trained to use the therapeutic model, tried to argue that counseling should not be subjected to the demands for accountability because it was a process, not a product. After all, how could you quantify insight and motivation? Recessions and deficits, however, have a way of bringing many important issues into focus. Counselors began to see that accountability was not just a passing whim; it was here to stay.

From a developmental perspective, counselors who respond to the call for accountability because it is imposed on them by a higher authority might be placed in the early stages of professional growth—what one might call the preoperations stage, to borrow from the wisdom of Piaget (1969). At this early level, external locus of control imposes its rules and sanctions on those who either need or allow themselves to be led by others. Counselors who assume more and more responsibility for developing their own programs and for demonstrating their worth to a critical public seem to move to a level in which intrinsic motivators predominate. At this level of "formal operations," counselors possess more of an internal locus of control and realize that they are primarily responsible for the success and acceptance of their programs. By embracing the concept of accountability, counselors then begin to assume tasks, promote change, and provide leadership. At the highest levels of this developmental continuum, counselors value the concept and nature of accountability and incorporate it into their daily performance in an almost automatic manner.

## ACTIVITY: ASKING WHY

**1.** Take a few moments to think about some of the Why questions that are surfacing in your own mind as you think about the role of the counseling profession and your work in the schools. We have generated our list of Why questions for you to ponder, but do not read our list until you have worked together in a small group to generate your own questions. Use the following space to list what you consider to be the most thought-provoking questions generated by your group.

2. Below is the beginning of our list of Why questions. Look them over and compare them with the list that your group generated. Feel free to add your own questions. The list is by no means exhaustive.

    **a.** Why should we hire another counselor?
    **b.** Why are so many students in need of individual counseling?
    **c.** Why should we be doing classroom guidance when so many kids are in need of individual counseling?
    **d.** Why are teachers reluctant to let counselors in their classrooms?
    **e.** Why don't administrators provide more support to counseling programs?
    **f.** Why are counseling positions some of the first to be cut when there is a budget crisis?
    **g.** Why can't counselors do what they enjoy most—and forget the rest?
    **h.** Why did I want to become a counselor in the first place?
    **i.** Why do so many counselors resist being good managers of their programs?
    **j.** Why do we need comprehensive K–12 developmental guidance and counseling programs?
    **k.** Why _____
    **l.** Why _____
    **m.** Why _____
    **n.** Why _____

**3.** What generalized messages can be gleaned from this exercise? What other questions need to be asked?

Now, we're pretty sure that you would appreciate it if we would just give you the answers to these questions so that you could get on with your life, but we couldn't make it that easy! Besides, there is no one right answer to each of those questions—nor will there be any simple reasons for most of the challenging questions that face counselors as they develop, implement, and revise their programs. The answers to the questions may vary because of circumstances, personalities, socioeconomic needs, structural boundaries, philosophies, theoretical persuasion, personal preferences, resources, higher-level thinking, creativity, education and training, politics, economics, and a variety of other variables.

We do believe, however, that students should spend some time trying to generate their own responses to these questions (and their own questions). Herein lies the significance of generating such a list: *In seeking and formulating the answers, you establish the purpose for your own behavior as a counselor.* Purposeful behavior is time well spent. If counselors don't know why they are taking on certain responsibilities or performing certain tasks, their motivation will more than likely be at a minimum. Furthermore, if in the process of seeking answers to the Why questions, counselors cannot rationalize their (or the program's) behavior, then they should abandon the tasks. With the thousands of things a counselor could be doing to fill a day's schedule, we certainly do not need to take on responsibilities for which there is very little purpose.

## DEFINING ACCOUNTABILITY

There are many definitions of accountability. We approach this definition more as a dissection activity in a biology class than as a dictionary activity in an

English class. Looking at the various compönents of the definition should help you appreciate the complexity of the concept and seek the identity and significance of its parts.

> Accountability is a condition…in which meaningful information…
> about program needs…and accomplishments…is made available…
> to those who are responsible for…or affected by the program…and
> avenues are accessible…for creating changes. (Wysong, 1973)

Because an understanding of accountability is the foundation for this handbook, we will explain each aspect of this statement.

## Accountability as a Condition

A condition is a state of existence created by various factors; it is pervasive rather than situational or isolated. A counselor cannot sit down one day and comply with accountability as if it were a task. Creating the condition of accountability takes time and thought; it entails conceptualizing and planning so that all those involved can agree on the factors that promote accountability and the kinds of responsibilities that must be assumed for those factors to be addressed.

## Meaningful Information

What makes information meaningful? What kinds of information are people looking for when they demand accountability? Are they looking for quantitative data that impress them with facts and figures? Do they value subjective comments? Will they understand the context in which any given accountability report is delivered? Will they be so critical of the way you present your program that they won't be able to look at your program's accomplishments? By identifying those who will receive the information, we should be able to see it from their perspective so that we can address their conceptualization of meaningfulness. If we understand the consumers of such information, we will more clearly understand how to make it meaningful.

## Program Needs

Identifying the areas of need that should be addressed in a guidance program is a major task. Despite years of training as a counselor, no one should rely solely on professional judgment in determining the priorities of the program. Seeking input from others is an important part of accountability and requires some fairly sophisticated skills. We'll help develop an appropriate level of sophistication in Chapter 4.

## Program Accomplishments

We need to promote our own program—to blow our own horns! We can't wait around for everyone to recognize all the good things we do; others are busy keeping up with all the good things they are doing. However, bragging about ourselves runs contrary to all those admonitions we were given as children. Nonetheless, if we recognize the importance of letting people know that we have been successful in addressing the needs we identified, then we must learn to brag with humility. Public relations is such an important topic that we are going to devote an entire chapter to it (Chapter 7).

## Availability

If we spend countless hours . . . days . . . weeks . . . compiling information about program needs and accomplishments, and the information sits on a shelf or hides in the recesses of a file drawer, we have wasted our time. We need to share the information and we need to give considerable thought to the most appropriate ways to make it available so that people really understand it and use it.

## Responsibility

We certainly need to feel responsible for our own programs. Does the responsibility end there, though? If we think more globally, we recognize that school principals feel responsible for all that goes on in their buildings, that school superintendents feel responsible for all the education programs in their districts, and that school board members feel responsible for representing the public's best interests. In a well-integrated program, we need to foster a sense of responsibility in classroom teachers, librarians, support staff, and others who contribute regularly to the objectives of our program. We can even make a case for Toni Taxpayer who is wondering whether her tax money is being spent for a worthwhile cause. We'll stop there, since we're sure you get the point. It is always important to remember, however, that those who feel responsible will most likely be more committed to and involved in the program.

## Beneficiaries

In looking at the people who benefit most from our guidance programs, we need once again to think globally. Students are the primary beneficiaries of our services, but parents and teachers should also be included as groups who benefit from our various roles. In a more indirect way, the community has much to gain from a strong guidance program. Is the same information meaningful to each of these groups?

## Accessible Avenues

We need to be creative in exploring opportunities for seeking and sharing information about guidance needs and accomplishments. Looking beyond the traditional end-of-the-year report, we should think about the different ways we like to receive information that piques our curiosity or motivates us in some way and turn that around to create avenues of communication.

## Change

Rarely does change come in a hurry. If we expect change to take place within the context of accountable guidance programs, we need to keep in mind all the facets of accountability and the many ways that change can take place. Steady improvement should be the kind of change we seek.

*ACTIVITY: PERSONALIZING ACCOUNTABILITY* _____

Now, without looking at what you just read (no peeking!), jot down the most important things you want to remember about accountability. Don't be limited by the definitions given above; personalize the meaning of accountability so that it becomes a definition you can use.

Next, working in your small groups and without looking at the definition that we have given, try to put together a "consensus" definition of accountability.

## DEFINING THE HUMAN FACTOR

Have you ever seen a program that looked really great on paper but fell flat because of the way it was run? To avoid that situation, we offer some advice about the balance necessary between management skills and people skills. Outstanding planning and implementation strategies may be rendered useless by inattention to the dynamics of what we refer to as the Human Factor. Managers of counseling programs must work to create a cooperative and inviting atmosphere within the school for school personnel, parents, community members, and most important, students. Human skills and an awareness of the human condition are essential ingredients in the overall development of the counseling program, the successful implementation of the many assigned responsibilities, and the direct delivery of counseling and consultation interventions.

The nature of the profession requires counselors to be attuned to individual differences among clients; likewise, they must also be aware of the differences among staff personnel and members of the public with whom they work.

They must also be honest and genuine in examining their own biases and issues that interfere with their ability to be totally objective and empathic. By understanding the issues that people bring to both the therapeutic and administrative aspects of the counseling program, counselors can become sensitive to the types of communication that will encourage receptivity and foster progress.

Most counselor education programs require at least some course work in the area referred to by the Council for the Accreditation of Counseling and Related Educational Programs (CACREP) as social and psychological foundations. An awareness of the basic tenets of sociology plus a firm grounding in developmental psychology (as well as other psychological theories) is considered basic to the development of counseling skills. Understanding people and how they seem to function, both individually and in groups, will be the daily challenge for every counselor for the rest of her or his professional life.

The most important Human Factor in an effective program is the counselor's personality. This is not to say there is one "counselor personality." On the contrary, the counseling profession needs diverse and unique personalities. But all counseling professionals must be committed to continual self-examination and ever-changing self-knowledge. Counselors must know what works for them individually, stylistically, theoretically, and emotionally if they are to be effective.

Sometimes we receive valuable feedback through instruments like the Myers-Briggs Type Indicator (MBTI) (Myers & Briggs, 1992) or the 16 Personality Factor Inventory (16PFI) (Cattell & Institute Staff, 1991). Such investigations can be enlightening. For example, if a counselor discovers that she is a strong I (Introvert) on the MBTI, she may better understand why classroom guidance responsibilities seem so challenging. With this knowledge, she may work harder to be more extraverted *in the classroom* to facilitate the motivation of students and to reach her goals.

The most challenging and sometimes most intimidating kind of feedback comes from friends and co-workers. They can be affirming in sharing perceptions of your best traits and behaviors, but if they are honest and candid, they will also point out those personal traits and behaviors that work to your disadvantage. Hearing similar comments from several people should help you form an accurate picture of how you are perceived. You can then use this information in positive ways to maximize your strengths and minimize your weaknesses.

As an example, a counselor went to three associates and asked them to list his most positive attributes and then to give him some honest feedback about his personal traits or habits that bothered them. He assured them that he welcomed their criticism because he was trying to improve his image with students and faculty. When he received their comments he was flattered about the many positive things his colleagues had to say about him but was surprised that two of his associates mentioned the clothes he wore as being his greatest deficit. Even the third associate confirmed that the way he dressed may have negatively affected the way he was perceived by students in particular. He was made aware that his clothes sometimes didn't match and that when he wore white socks to school, the students made jokes about it. As a result, the counselor bought a book on men's fashions. Later, however, he confided to his colleague that he really didn't like the fashions he saw in the book, and besides, he couldn't afford such clothes with his salary. The colleague decided to spend a Saturday at the local mall with this counselor to point out the basic rules of selecting clothes and to suggest some other alterations in his professional appearance. After changing the way he dressed the counselor began to feel more confident about how he was perceived by his students and his peers. He realized that even though it was a little disconcerting to have people tell him he did not dress well he was glad they had been candid enough to help him change in a positive way.

Of course, all the feedback we receive cannot be as tangible or as non-threatening as discovering that we need a new wardrobe. However, if we really believe in the importance of the Human Factor in the success of our school counseling programs, then we need to be open-minded and receptive to feedback from others.

### ACTIVITY: GETTING TO KNOW YOU ────────────────────

**1.** Choose one other member of your class and spend a maximum of 10 minutes each describing what you perceive to be the major problems with today's school counseling programs. Write down five or six of these.

**2.** Next, spend about five minutes contemplating and providing written feedback to your partner in response to the following questions:

**a.** What three adjectives would you use to describe me?

_____    _____    _____

**b.** If I were your counselor, is there anything about me that would make it difficult for you to talk with me?

**c.** If you were the superintendent of schools and I were interviewing for a counseling position in your district, what would you consider to be my assets as a candidate, and what would you consider to be my deficits?

**d.** Ask for responses to the same questions from a family member or close friend.

*ACTIVITY: GETTING TO KNOW YOURSELF* —————————————

Take a personality test and ask for a thorough interpretive report.

*ACTIVITY: EXPLORING THE HUMAN FACTOR* —————————————

In a small group, explore the significance of the Human Factor in the overall functioning of a successful school counseling program.

We will remind you of the Human Factor throughout this handbook because it is embedded in every aspect of a comprehensive guidance and counseling program. We have discussed it in this chapter because we want you to consider it an essential ingredient in the refinement of any model you choose for developing a comprehensive school counseling program.

**SUMMARY**

In this chapter, we have given the "Why" of the handbook. In succeeding chapters, we will help you with the "How." Keep in mind that the handbook is intended to assist you in applying the theory and practice that you will learn from textbooks and supplementary readings. We are attempting to help you conceptualize comprehensive, developmental school guidance and counseling. This handbook is a blueprint to enable you, the prospective counselor, to try out some major concepts and to put them into their appropriate perspectives.

## REFLECTIONS ON CHAPTER 1

**1.** What Was It Like to Work in a Small Group? _____

_____

_____

_____

_____

_____

**2.** What Challenged You Most in Your Group Activity? _____

_____

_____

_____

_____

_____

**3.** How Do You Feel about Your Role in Your Group? _____

_____

_____

_____

_____

_____

**4.** What Questions Do You Have for Yourself, Your Group Members, or Your Instructor? _____

_____

_____

_____

_____

_____

**5.** How Do You Feel about the Importance of the Topic of Accountability for Your Preparation? _____

_____

_____

_____

_____

_____

**6.** Notes _____

_____

_____

_____

_____

# CHAPTER **2**

# Conceptualizing the Program

Students in counselor education programs need to experience the development of comprehensive guidance and counseling programs from the beginning struggle to the final product. This chapter provides an opportunity for you to identify with various perspectives that contribute to the development of a total program. We will provide you with learning activities, such as brainstorming and flowcharting skills, that will help you conceptualize the program.

## SEEING THE BIG PICTURE

*Seeing the Big Picture* means having a broad view of the total undertaking and is fundamental to creating and maintaining a program that is truly comprehensive and developmental. Seeing this way involves higher-level thinking, comprehension, and the ability to synthesize. Counselors with this kind of vision can take an ill-defined conglomeration of tasks and activities, and mold them into a well-integrated program.

Seeing the Big Picture is another way of talking about *systems thinking*. In this handbook we will not probe deeply into systems analysis, but we will introduce you to some basic systems concepts that will help you lay the foundation for sound program management practices. Essentially, a *system* is a structure whose orderly whole comprises integral parts (subsystems) that function together to accomplish a specific mission.

## *ACTIVITY: MAKING SENSE OF SYSTEMS*

In your groups, investigate *each* concept in the definition given above. Keeping in mind the enormous task of developing a K–12 comprehensive, developmental school counseling program, discuss the implications of the following questions:

1. What do we mean by *structure*?
2. What is an *orderly whole*?
3. What are integral parts or *subsystems*?
4. What is the significance of the term *function together*?
5. How does the term *accomplish* fit into the definition of a system?
6. What do we mean by *mission*?

After discussing the concepts, have at least one member of the group describe a system in lay terms.

One of the outstanding characteristics of a system is that it fosters "intentional achievement." If your goal is to have an excellent school counseling program, it is imperative for you to create a process that enables you to reach that goal in the most efficient and responsible manner.


## DEVELOPING A FLOWCHART

One of the more useful tools for conceptualizing a system is the *flowchart*. Even though many flowcharts are as complex as the circuit board of a transistor radio, we nonetheless have grown to appreciate them for the way they help us see the big picture. One of the most beneficial aspects of developing and using a flowchart is that everyone involved in a project has the same visual picture of the system they are all working in.

Flowcharts created by big business are often complex and filled with technical jargon, but charts can be much simpler. Here we give you a slimmed-down, user-friendly version that employs a limited number of guidelines.

Most of you have had to create an outline at various times in your life. (You know the rules: Each major heading starts with a Roman numeral, the subcategories under that start with a capital letter, you must have at least two entries in each category, and so on.) Flowcharting is very much like doing an outline. One nice thing about the flowchart is that it usually can be displayed on a single piece of paper.

There are key terms to remember in creating a flowchart:

1. Function Box
2. Function Code
3. Descriptors
4. Signal Paths
5. Cumulation Dots
6. Feedback Loops
7. Feed Forward Loops

Follow along as we explain these terms.

## Function Box

Each major part or function of any system is entitled to a prominent place that highlights its significance (similar to any heading that is worthy of a Roman numeral in an outline). To illustrate with a simple example, if your goal is to bake a cake for a special occasion, there are four major functions to consider. These are illustrated in the *function boxes* in Figure 2.1.

Later, when the flowchart becomes more sophisticated, we need to include subfunctions in each of the function boxes. For example, under the "Prepare cake" function, there are subfunctions such as Read recipe, Purchase ingredients, Pre-heat oven, Mix cake. Take a moment to list some of the subfunctions that would be listed in each of the function boxes in Figure 2.1.

**FIGURE 2.1**   Function boxes

| Prepare cake | Bake cake | Clean up | Serve cake |

## Function Code

Most projects have a sequential order; one thing must be done before the next thing can be accomplished. In Figure 2.1, the first two functions have an obvious sequence; the last two may be interchanged, depending on the baker's style (some put off the cleaning part as long as they can). However, assuming that cleaning up should be done before the cake is served, we then have an order to our actions. To denote the order of events, we assign *function codes*, which provide a numerical sequence (Figure 2.2). Thus, our flowchart takes on a new look.

**FIGURE 2.2**   Flowchart with function codes

| Prepare cake | Bake cake | Clean up | Serve cake |
| 1.0 | 2.0 | 3.0 | 4.0 |

## Descriptors

So that everyone uses a common style of language, we suggest that you use action verbs to describe each function. Also, you need to state the function as clearly and concisely as possible so that everyone using the flowchart has the common understanding required for intentional achievement to take place. Try to limit *descriptors* to five words or fewer. Thus, the flowchart takes on a slightly new appearance (see Figure 2.3).

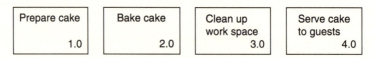

**FIGURE 2.3**   Flowchart with descriptors

## Signal Paths

To find your way on any map, you need to have a sense of direction or some clear signals that direct your way. Signal paths are arrows that show the exact route to take in progressing through the flowchart. A new dimension is added in Figure 2.4 to illustrate the *signal paths*.

**FIGURE 2.4**   Flowchart with signal paths

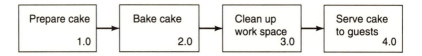

## Cumulation Dots

When several subfunctions within a function box must all be done, but in no particular order, they are marked with a *cumulation dot*. Thus, in our confectionery example, if the Clean up function requires the subfunctions of Soak pans, Throw away paper products, and Clear counter space, there is no particular order for which subfunction must be done first. The function box would look like Figure 2.5.

**FIGURE 2.5**   Flowchart with cumulation dots

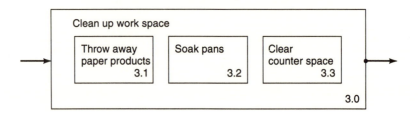

## Feedback Loops

When a decision in one function box relies on information from a previous box or results in a changed procedure in that previous box, we use a *feedback loop*, denoted by Ⓕ.

For example, if you want to rate the cake's quality, you may want to have a fifth function box that becomes a decision box. It would look like Figure 2.6.

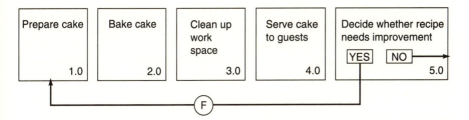

**FIGURE 2.6**  Flowchart with feedback loop

## Feed Forward Loops

Essentially, the feed forward loop allows you to skip a step or two in a normally sequential routine. We know we have beaten this cake to death, but we will use one more example (Figure 2.7) before it is totally stale.

You can see from Figure 2.7 that decision function boxes often generate variable routes of action. In looking at all the steps, we have discovered that it is not just a single four-step process; we have expanded it to several possible functions that are fairly distinct and really quite complex.

Later, when you explore some of the major functions of a comprehensive, developmental school guidance and counseling program, we hope you *won't*

**FIGURE 2.7**  Flowchart with feed forward loop

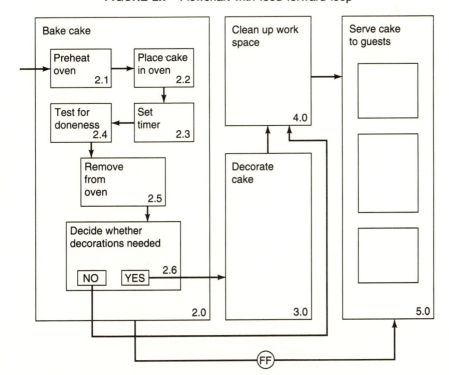

spend time on minutiae like "Fill the coffee pot" under the function of "Conduct steering committee meetings." We've led you through this rather detailed cooking lesson to demonstrate the importance of seeing how things function together to make a whole. The skills of analyzing and synthesizing, if learned well, may empower you for the rest of your life as they help you envision the entire program and all its parts.

## ACTIVITY: DEVELOPING A FLOWCHART: TRIAL RUN ——————

In small groups, choose one of the following three projects:

1. Plan a party
2. Plan how you will write a term paper
3. Plan a trip

Design a flowchart to illustrate the sequence of your plan. It should take 20–30 minutes to generate a "rough" flowchart that generally depicts your group's version of the Big Picture and its parts.

Describe your plan/flowchart to the rest of the class. Also, describe the process your group used to plan.

Discuss what you have learned about systems thinking.

If you have done a really good job, why not carry out your plan—especially if your group chose option 1.

Now, you are ready to form the groups with which you will be working for the next several weeks in the planning of a comprehensive, developmental school counseling and guidance program. Group cooperation and teamwork are essential, so focus your energy on making this group experience one of the most important learning opportunities of your professional life.

## ACTIVITY: ASSUMING ROLES

Divide the class into two planning groups—or three if you are in a particularly large class. Each member of each group assumes the role of a member of the school or community. Some suggested roles are principal, head counselor, counselor, media specialist, curriculum coordinator, classroom teacher, secretary, member of the business community, parent, or student. After each class member has stated the role that he or she is assuming, the group should spend the next few minutes brainstorming the various perspectives each of the role players might bring to the group. *Even though each group member will be assuming equal responsibility for the group's task, he or she should always try to infuse some of the typical thinking and contributions that might be offered by the person he or she is representing as a team member.*

Since we suggest several activities that involve brainstorming, we will list the basic rules of brainstorming here as a reference for your use. Carefully observe these rules as you seek input from your groups, since brainstorming is a key concept in planning and needs to be respected.

1. One or two people should take responsibility for writing everything down, preferably on a chalkboard or on newsprint.
2. Any idea, no matter how unusual, should be voiced.
3. Build on one another's ideas.
4. Every idea is as good as every other idea—no put downs.
5. Do not analyze or critique any suggestions during brainstorming; save that until all ideas are recorded.

## APPLYING GROUP PROCESS SKILLS

Perhaps one of your first thoughts is, "Wouldn't it be easier if the counselor just wrote the plan and then handed it out to all these people?" We submit that doing the work yourself may be quicker and easier, but it probably will not be better . . . and it certainly will not represent the collective thinking of important people who are affected by or responsible for the program (remember the definition of accountability?).

Sharing the leadership and the responsibility for developing and implementing a guidance and counseling program takes longer and is a little harder to do. It is also more interesting and can be a lot more fun. However, the key to making this group experience a worthwhile venture lies in everyone having a fundamental understanding of group process. We will provide you with a rather cursory overview of group process and encourage you to find other sources that can assist you in getting all group members to contribute in meaningful ways to the group's task *and* process. One of the most important lessons to learn about groups, though, is that they move in and out of stages. There are usually four stages of group process: *forming, storming, norming*, and *performing*.

The *forming stage* is often referred to as a time for getting acquainted. It is essentially an effort to gather people together for a common—but often nebulous—purpose.

The *storming stage* is not always stormy, but it can be unsettling. At this stage, group participants are seeking purpose, clarity of mission, direction, and security in their group. Often, members will consciously or unconsciously assert the roles they hope to play in the group. It is also a time when group members are trying to decide whether they want to be or will be committed to the group's mission.

More than any other time in the group's development, this is a time for strong group facilitation skills and a time for *communication*. The storminess of this stage is often misunderstood, and people abandon the group because they do not think people can get along or because it seems too chaotic. Understanding that this behavior is normal and necessary can give group members hope that, out of storming, group cohesiveness and a common effort are attainable.

The *norming stage* starts evolving as leadership begins to emerge. Once group members understand the mission and see the work as possible and plausible, they often volunteer for tasks in which their strengths will surface. A game plan is set, and sometimes rules or procedures are established for maintaining focus and civility.

The *performing stage* is also referred to as the working stage. Because group members understand the parameters of their assignment and have agreed to group norms, they feel comfortable in accomplishing group tasks.

Groups often move sequentially through these stages at varying speeds of efficiency, depending on group needs. However, once the groups have reached the performing stage, they can also expect to revisit earlier stages on a regular basis. A good group facilitator will recognize the time to move to another stage (either forward or reverse), or will be able to see when the group has moved to another stage and will deal with the transition accordingly. Experience tells us that creating a comprehensive, developmental school counseling program plan will move among two or more stages *every time you meet*, and that is why it is necessary to assess *continuously* how your cooperative learning group is doing.

## *ACTIVITY: DEVELOPING A FLOWCHART PROTOTYPE* ──────

You are now going to begin work on a flowchart for developing a comprehensive school guidance and counseling program that represents the thinking of your small group. Without looking ahead to future chapters, use the blank flowchart in Figure 2.8 and the list of major functions that follows to create a sequence of functions that might represent a tentative district plan for a comprehensive, developmental school counseling and guidance program. This flowchart will become your working model. You will probably change it somewhat as you gain new knowledge of the functions and activities needed for planning and implementing a comprehensive school counseling and guid-

**FIGURE 2.8** Blank flowchart for planning a comprehensive guidance and counseling program. Identify major functions, assign subfunctions, and draw in signal paths.

ance program. However, your task in this activity is to begin the "sorting out" stage of conceptualizing the Big Picture.

You do not have to use all the boxes—or you may choose to add more or enlarge some. Your task as a group is to use the following major functions to *create a flowchart that you believe will determine the sequence that will move your group toward the development of a comprehensive school counseling and guidance program.*

### Major Functions (in alphabetical order)

Assign responsibilities

Conceptualize the program

Conduct program research and evaluation

Determine program priorities

Develop public relations strategies

Establish program leadership and supervision

Examine program models

Identify needs

Organize program support

Refine the model

You have (tentatively) created the basic flowchart that you will use throughout this process for envisioning your program. Congratulations on becoming a systems thinker! Now, assign some of the subfunctions to their appropriate function boxes.

### Subfunctions (in random order)

Select advisory committee

Prepare budget

Develop counselor evaluation

Disseminate results

Review established models

Adopt evaluation plan

Explore grant writing

Address the Human Factor

Identify individual leadership strengths

Identify program coordinator

Identify resources

Plan inservice education

Plan for peer supervision

Complete professional development plans

Identify professional growth opportunities

Establish program/clinical supervision

Explore program considerations

Design program evaluation

Develop public relations plan

Publish articles

Identify research projects

Create skill-building activities

Suggest changes in program

## *ACTIVITY: PLAN THE PLAN*

Now that you have the Big Picture in mind, you have a sense of the task before you. In the weeks ahead, your group needs to generate the substantive content that will build on the foundation provided by the flowchart and demonstrate in what ways your plan is truly *comprehensive* and *developmental*.

**1.** Your group's task at this point is to return once again to brainstorming. Spend about 10 minutes naming as many things as you can think of that must be accomplished for your group to ultimately make a presentation to the other group(s) in class (who will be acting as a school board), where you will unveil your own comprehensive, developmental school guidance and counseling program plan.

**2.** Take your brainstormed ideas and use them to develop a new flow-chart, illustrating how your group will function in the weeks ahead. It is usually a good idea to determine what you want your final product or task to be and then work back to what you must do first. Everything in between needs to be sequenced to take you step-by-step to a successful fulfillment of your plan. Be as detailed as you need to be. Keep in mind that there may be both task and maintenance roles, as explained in Figure 2.9, that may need attention as you proceed in this group effort.

## *ACTIVITY: UNDERSTANDING ROLE FUNCTIONS IN YOUR GROUP*

After having worked together in your small group for even a short amount of time, it is important to pause and reflect on the group process that is already underway. This role function analysis should not be confused with the character roles you are playing in your groups. Rather, this analysis is examining the interpersonal and facilitative roles that are starting to surface as you interact with one another. For example, some group members may have argued strong-

**FIGURE 2.9** Role functions in a group

SOURCE: Reprinted from J. William Pfeiffer and John E. Jones (Eds.), 1976, *The 1976 Annual Handbook for Group Facilitators*, San Diego, CA: Pfeiffer & Company. Used with permission.

The members of an efficient and productive group must provide for meeting two kinds of needs—what it takes to do the job, and what it takes to strengthen and maintain the group. What members do to serve group needs may be called functional roles. Statements and behaviors which tend to make the group inefficient or weak may be called nonfunctional behaviors.

A partial list of the kinds of contributions or the group services that are performed by one or many individuals is as follows:

A. **Task Roles**  (functions required in selecting and carrying out a group task)
   1. *Initiating Activity:* Proposing solutions, suggesting new ideas, new definitions of the problem, new attack on the problem, or new organization of material.
   2. *Seeking Information:* Asking for clarification or suggestions, requesting additional information or facts.
   3. *Seeking Opinion:* Looking for an expression of feeling about something from the members, seeking clarification of values, suggestions, or ideas.
   4. *Giving Information:* Offering facts or generalizations, relating one's experience to the group problem to illustrate points.
   5. *Giving Opinion:* Stating an opinion or belief concerning a suggestion or one of several suggestions, particularly concerning its value rather than its factual basis.
   6. *Elaborating:* Clarifying, giving examples or developing meanings, trying to envision how a proposal might work if adopted.
   7. *Coordinating:* Showing relationships among various ideas or suggestions, trying to pull ideas and suggestions together.
   8. *Summarizing:* Pulling together related suggestions or ideas, restating suggestions after the group has discussed them.
B. **Group Building and Maintenance Roles**   (functions required in strengthening and maintaining group life and activities)
   1. *Encouraging:* Being friendly, warm, responsive to others, praising others and their ideas, agreeing with and accepting contributions of others.
   2. *Gatekeeping:* Trying to make it possible for another to make a contribution to the group by saying, "We haven't heard from Jim yet" or suggesting limited talking time for everyone so that all will have a chance to be heard.
   3. *Standard Setting:* Expressing standards for the group to use in choosing its content or procedures or in evaluating its decisions, reminding group to avoid decisions that conflict with group standards.
   4. *Following:* Going along with decisions of the group, thoughtfully accepting ideas of others, serving as audience during group discussion.
   5. *Expressing Group Feeling:* Summarizing what group feeling is sensed to be, describing reactions of the group to ideas or solutions.
C. **Both Group Task and Maintenance Roles**
   1. *Evaluating:* Submitting group decisions or accomplishments to comparison with group standards, measuring accomplishments against goals.
   2. *Diagnosing:* Determining sources of difficulties, appropriate steps to take next, analyzing the main blocks to progress.
   3. *Testing for Consensus:* Tentatively asking for group opinions in order to find out whether the group is reaching consensus on a decision, sending up trial balloons to test group opinions.

4. *Mediating:* Harmonizing, conciliating differences in points of view, making compromise solutions.
5. *Relieving Tension:* Draining off negative feeling by jesting or pouring oil on troubled waters, putting a tense situation in wider context.

D. **Types of Nonfunctional Behavior**
1. *Being Aggressive:* Working for status by criticizing or blaming others, showing hostility against the group or some individual, deflating the ego or status of others.
2. *Blocking:* Interfering with the progress of the group by going off on a tangent, citing personal experiences unrelated to the problem, arguing too much on a point, rejecting ideas without consideration.
3. *Self-Confessing:* Using the group as a sounding board, expressing personal, nongroup-oriented feelings or points of view.
4. *Competing:* Vying with others to produce the best idea, talk the most, play the most roles, gain favor with the leader.
5. *Seeking Sympathy:* Trying to induce other members of the group to be sympathetic to one's problems or misfortunes, deploring one's own situation, or disparaging one's own ideas to gain support.
6. *Special Pleading:* Introducing or supporting suggestions relating to one's own pet concerns or philosophies, lobbying.
7. *Horsing Around:* Clowning, joking, mimicking, disrupting the work of the group.
8. *Seeking Recognition:* Attempting to call attention to one's self by loud or excessive talking, extreme ideas, unusual behavior.
9. *Withdrawal:* Acting indifferent or passive, resorting to excessive formality, daydreaming, doodling, whispering to others, wandering from the subject.

In using this or any other classification, people need to guard against the tendency to blame any person (whether themselves or another) who falls into "nonfunctional behavior." It is more useful to regard such behavior as a symptom that all is not well with the group's ability to satisfy individual needs through group centered activity. People need to be alert to the fact that each person is likely to interpret such behaviors differently. What appears to be nonfunctional behavior may not be necessarily so, for the content and the group conditions must also be taken into account.

E. **Improving Member Roles** Any group is strengthened and enabled to work more efficiently if its members:
1. become more conscious of the role function needed at any given time;
2. become more sensitive to and aware of the degree to which they can help to meet the needs through what they do;
3. undertake self-training to improve their range of role functions and skills in performing them.

ly for a particular placement of an item on one of the flowcharts. Others may have disagreed but gone along with the majority opinion. Others may have been passive participants. This activity provides you with an opportunity to analyze the strengths and needs of your group as a whole, and of individual members of the group.

Using Figure 2.9, identify the role functions that the individuals in your group are playing. Attach some "tentative" labels to group members. Should these labels be discussed or explored at this time, or monitored for future reference? What functions are missing that someone needs to add? Are non-functional behaviors already getting in the way of your group's effectiveness? Do you need to promote a certain role for someone within your group that will improve your group's effectiveness?

Assess whether you used *your* best communication skills: clearly articulating your position, accurately and sensitively listening to others, reading the nonverbal signals of other group members, and using graphic or written information when it assisted in promoting understanding. If you are trying to practice better group skills or feel that your contributions are not valued by the group, take this opportunity to share your needs.

Be sure to share what you like about your group, as well as your concerns at this point. Come back to this activity from time to time. Your careful attention to the group process at work in your group is a critical feature of this handbook. If you learn the substantive lessons of group process, you will gain an extremely significant skill for working with a team of counselors and co-workers to create quality school guidance and counseling programs. As a future change agent in the schools, you will also be learning skills that will assist schools in such efforts as school restructuring and site-based management.

## *ACTIVITY: ASSUMING AND ASSIGNING RESPONSIBILITY* _____

**1.** As an extension of the Activity "Plan the Plan," you may want to assign members of your group to assume responsibility for various tasks that have been identified through your brainstorming and refinement efforts. Sharing the load is important. You will need to provide ample opportunity for group members to share their accomplishments and to ask questions that will assure everyone that you are all headed in the same direction.

**2.** Now that you have all had an opportunity to observe each other within your group and perhaps name the roles people are bringing to the group process, we have two major decisions that your group must make that could have a significant impact on the final product you produce. You need to name a director of guidance and a scribe.

The choice of director of guidance makes a statement about the kind of leadership your group either needs or allows itself to be influenced by. We usually encourage people to campaign for this position. It allows people to assert themselves and to highlight their leadership skills. Often, groups take an extra week to decide on this important position because it gives people the chance to think about the significance of the choice or the potential for personal growth and the decision to campaign for the job or not. Every group member should be asking, "What kind of leader does this group need?" Ultimately, the group decides, and you need to make choices about whether the final decision is by majority rule, consensus, or default.

The scribe position is extremely important, as well. It has been said that the most powerful member of any committee is its secretary. What gets recorded and how it is recorded are fundamental to the final reports that surface from any group. If the final product is fraught with spelling and grammatical errors and omissions, it is a reflection on the group making the report. Therefore, your group's scribe should be able to convince you that her or his word processing skills are exemplary and that the final product of your group will make everyone proud!

Ultimately, every group member needs to share personal strengths that contribute to the group's mission. Once again, a chain is only as strong as its weakest link.

## SUMMARY

This chapter has discussed some of the fundamental skills you will need to adequately plan and ultimately implement a guidance plan that is holistic, sequential, focused, integrated, and accountable. You may need to spend more than one week exploring the many activities in this chapter, and you may need to return to them to refocus your group's efforts. Discover where the feedback loops are needed and return to this chapter to get back on track as any good systems thinker would do.

## REFLECTIONS ON CHAPTER 2

**1.** How Do You Feel about the Group's Task? _____

_____

_____

_____

_____

_____

**2.** What's Going on in Your Group? _____

_____

_____

_____

_____

_____

**3.** How Do You Feel about the Progress of Your Group? _____

_____

_____

_____

_____

_____

**4.** How Do You Feel about Your Role in Your Group? _____

_____

_____

_____

_____

_____

**5.** What Questions Do You Have for Yourself, Your Group Members, or Your Instructor? _____

_____

_____

_____

_____

_____

**6.** Notes _____

_____

_____

_____

_____

# CHAPTER **3**

# Examining Program Models

Few topics are as important to school counselors as how to organize their guidance programs. . . . When school guidance and counseling is organized to meet specific goals and objectives and careful attention is directed towards "who will accomplish what," the evidence suggests that both the deliverers (counselors and school faculty) and students and parents are more satisfied. (Gysbers, Hughey, Starr, & Lapan, 1992)

We will not detail all the models for developing comprehensive school guidance and counseling programs except to refer you to the texts that are being used in our respective courses. Gysbers and Henderson's *Developing and Managing Your School Guidance Program* (1988) is the text in use at Plymouth State, and Myrick's *Developmental Guidance and Counseling* (1993) is used at the University of Southern Maine. These texts are highly respected by counselor educators and practitioners. Our expectation is that by the time you have completed the procedures and activities in this handbook, you will have developed a program that incorporates the best of each of these texts.

## THE NEW HAMPSHIRE AND MAINE MODELS

It is important to have, and perhaps to display where all can see, a model that becomes the center of attention of your program. We will explain two models that are being successfully used in most parts of the United States. These models are patterned after other existing models, especially the Missouri (Gysbers) model, and they have been developed and are being implemented by local, regional, and state practitioners.

We have included two graphic representations that we will refer to throughout this chapter. Figure 3.1 represents the New Hampshire model's adaptation of the Missouri model and Figure 3.2 represents a multidimensional model developed by VanZandt. These are included to help you understand that developing and delivering comprehensive guidance and counseling is complex and multidimensional.

## PROGRAM CONSIDERATIONS

For decades, a majority of counselor education programs trained counselors to use a therapeutic model within the public elementary and secondary schools. Counselors in training learned, and learned well, to counsel students one-on-one. Often, they would then take a job in a school system where they were

**FIGURE 3.1**    Adaptation of the Missouri model as used in the New Hampshire model

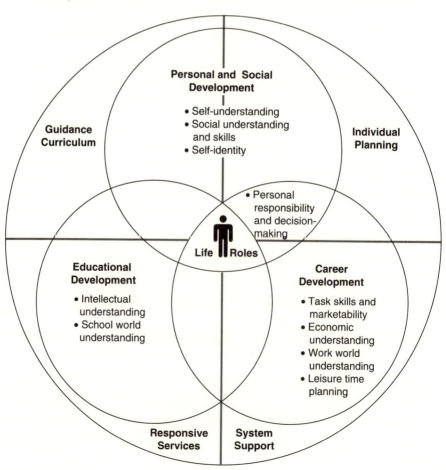

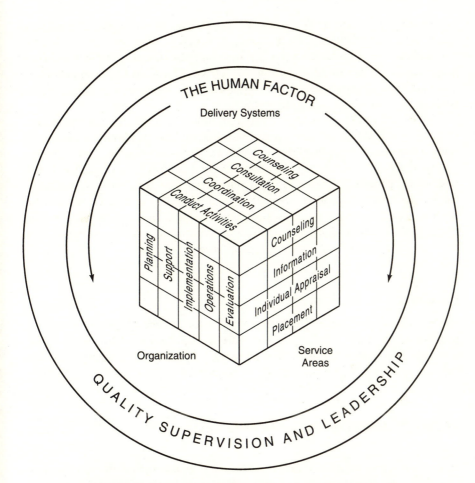

**FIGURE 3.2** Multidimensional model of guidance program management

expected to "hit the ground running," and to deliver guidance activities as expected of them by a harassed principal and/or board of education.

If these counselors had gone to large schools, they might have been hired to be the "adjustment" counselors, and indeed might have been able to work with individual clients. If they located in medium-sized schools, they were probably expected to provide a number of different services, including college counseling, career counseling, referral, and follow-up. More often than not, these new graduates found themselves in a one-counselor school where they were expected to carry out all the services and programs usually conducted by an experienced guidance director. These new counselors might have had a course in organization and administration of guidance programs, but the course was probably not a major emphasis in a total program that emphasized therapeutic counseling.

In the 1970s and 1980s, many counselor education programs began to move from a therapeutic or medical model, which delivers services to specific populations, to a comprehensive or developmental model, which delivers programs to all the students within the school. The need for an appropriate organizational structure that provides guidance and counseling programs to all students was finally being addressed.

In 1978, Gysbers described a program model that was the foundation for this new emphasis on guidance and counseling integrated into the total educational program of the school district. This emphasis defines the competencies that students develop through participation in a comprehensive guidance and counseling program. These competencies drive the total program and are carried with the students as they become adults. The competencies can be achieved in a number of ways programmatically. They all fit within four component areas: *guidance curriculum, individual planning, responsive services, and system support* or *program management*.

## Guidance Curriculum

The *guidance curriculum* provides a vehicle for delivering guidance content to all students in a systematic manner. After completing a school and communitywide needs assessment, school personnel are aware of guidance curriculum needs and can plan an organized, sequential way of addressing these.

## *ACTIVITY: IDENTIFYING COMPETENCIES* _____

As a group, on newsprint or on the chalkboard, brainstorm a list of competencies that you believe students need before they leave high school. Identify which of these competencies (1) can be taught by a classroom teacher as part of a course, (2) can be learned within a family or community setting separate from the school, or (3) can be team taught by a counselor and a teacher within a classroom or small group. Discuss the role of the counselor in each of these situations. Also, identify the earliest grade in a K–12 system in which the competency could (or should) be addressed.

## Individual Planning

*Individual planning* addresses the process of helping students develop their own life plans to reach their fullest potential. Methods used include individual appraisal, individual assessment, and placement. Individual planning does not necessarily mean that the counselor meets with the student one-on-one. It does mean that the best method of meeting with individual students is used. Often this is within a classroom or with a group of peers.

## *ACTIVITY: DETERMINING THE BEST SETTING* ————————

As a class, divide into three groups and develop lists of individual planning needs of students. Use individual appraisal, individual advisement, and placement as general headings. Identify as many activities as you can in which appraisal, advisement, and placement occur within the school. Label each as an one-on-one, a small group, or a classroom activity.

## Responsive Services

Counselors traditionally are trained to respond to students' needs, whether the students are in crisis or simply seeking information. The *responsive services* component of this program goes beyond the counseling expertise of the counselor and reaches out to the helping expertise of the faculty, the administration, and others who have skills that lend themselves to counseling in a school setting. In Maine and New Hampshire, for example, many classroom teachers and some administrators have earned certification as school counselors but have chosen to use their skills in classrooms or in the principal's office.

The emphasis on responsive services in this model is on prevention as well as intervention. Whether the counselor is working with an individual, a small group, or in a classroom, problem-solving and decision-making skills are emphasized so that students develop coping skills they can use in a variety of settings.

## *ACTIVITY: THE SOLUTION-BASED MODEL* ————————

The Solution-Based Model, Figure 3.3, is a good method for working with a student in a responsive services mode. Using the Solution-Based Model, create a responsive services scenario with which the school counselor is likely to be presented. Working in triads, one person becomes the counselor, one the student, and one the teacher or parent. Work for approximately 20 minutes to resolve the presenting problem.

Be aware that in creating your responsive services component, you need to develop and keep an up-to-date list of available referral programs, services, and individual providers. In the courses we teach, we require that students begin to create a file of resources they find valuable as they begin their practica or internships. This "Goodie File" requirement is described in the course outline—Appendix A.

## System Support/Program Management

*System support* or *program management*, sometimes considered the core of a guidance director's responsibility and sometimes considered a necessary evil,

**FIGURE 3.3** A school interview in two parts

SOURCE: J. K. Gilkey and I. K. Berg, 1991, *A School Interview in Two Parts: The Solution-Based Model*, Milwaukee, WI: Brief Family Therapy Center. Reprinted with permission of the authors.

---

### The Solution-Based Model

This format can be used with teachers and students, parents and students, and administrators and students. What follows is a format for a solution-based interview that we have found useful with "problem" children and whoever made the referral. The interview with the child usually takes about 20 minutes; the interview with the referring person usually takes about 5–10 minutes and can be done over the phone or in person.

Basic assumptions of the Solution-Based Model:

- Accept the view of the student as reality for him/her.
- Flow with that view.
- Name the problem that has to be solved.
- Search for exceptions to the problem condition.
- Use exceptions to find solutions.
- Compliment the student for willingness to confront the problem by talking to you and for any effort made toward solving the problem already.
- Compliment the referral person for hard work on the problem so far. (For involuntary clients: Who made you come here? What do they say has to be different?)

*Part 1 (With student)*

1. What has to be different as a result of you talking with me? What is your goal?

2. What is the last time you did this even a little bit better than now? (Ask this several times)

3. What were you doing differently at that time? (Need several answers to this question)

4. On a scale of 1 to 10, with 1 being not so sure and 10 being very sure, how sure are you that you could do some of these things again if you really wanted to?

5. How likely is it that you will be able to do some of these things again?

*Part 2 (With parent, teacher, etc.)*

1. Acknowledge their hard work on problem so far, dedication to solve problem, etc. What's the minimal change you can accept from this child?

2. When was the last time you found this child doing just a little bit better or a little more of what you wanted?

3. What was this child doing differently at that time? (Need several answers to this question)

4. What do you think you were doing that helped this child to do better at times? (Several answers) What would the child say you were doing that helped him/her at the time?

5. How willing are you to do these helpful things to help this child again?

After we have interviewed each party involved in the problem, we accept each person's view of the problem as reality for him/her and we compliment each on their efforts to solve the problem thus far. We refrain from making judgments on how that's been done. We then give each a task to do; if each has tried several things that have worked in part, we send them out to do more of those things and to come back or call and tell us how those worked.

If nothing has worked even a little bit or not too many things have worked, we send each party out to study themselves to see what works better in the next few days or a week. We then see them again or talk with them to get this information.

*Trust the pace and the path of the client.*

is as important as the other components. Often it is considered narrowly as the day-to-day operation of the guidance area. It includes but is not limited to research and development, public relations, professional development, committees and advisory boards, and community outreach. Counselors need a good grasp of program management to maintain inner control of their services. The person designated as the head counselor or guidance director should take the lead responsibility for convening the counselors on a regular basis to maintain communication among them and between them and other professionals.

## *ACTIVITY: SCHOOL BOARD SUMMONS* ———————————

Your local school board has requested a description of counselor activities for the previous academic year. You suspect that the board's motive is to cut one of the four positions in your district program, which has one elementary counselor K–6, two secondary school counselors 7–12, and one school adjustment counselor K–12. School enrollment K–12 is 1,200 students and growing by about 25 students per year. Base your presentation to the school board on an analysis of the time spent by guidance personnel on various activities. This is sometimes referred to as a time and task analysis. Use whatever support or information you can from other individuals in your school and community.

Process this activity: Ask the following questions in your group:

1. Without keeping records, how easy is it to explain how a counselor spends his or her time?
2. Considering the amount of time you suggested was being spent on various activities, how impressed do you think the school board would be? Why?

## THE MULTIDIMENSIONAL MODEL

In Chapter 1 we asked you to continually include the Human Factor as you plan and implement your comprehensive school guidance and counseling program. As you examine the multidimensional model (Figure 3.2), remember that the most important parts of any program are the human beings for whom the program is designed. The multidimensional model illustrates that the Human Factor is the glue that keeps the system together.

### Organization

The organizational design is the counselor's method of envisioning and depicting the finished product or the optimally functioning program before encountering the first student. It is a work design or operational structure that helps improve productivity.

The   Planning-Supporting-Implementing-Operating-Evaluating   (PSIOE) design illustrated in the lower left part of the cube in Figure 3.2 is an organizational format suggested by the national project entitled "Legislative Provisions for the Development of Comprehensive Community-Based Career Guidance Programs" (Drier, Jones, & Jones, 1985). The PSIOE format provides a comprehensive framework in which to envision program organization.

## Delivery Systems

With each new professional encounter, a counselor must determine the most appropriate intervention strategy. Counselors don't "just do counseling." Since the mid-1960s, counselors have been indoctrinated with the thinking that the "Three C's" constituted the major functions performed by a counselor (counseling, consultation, and coordination). The multidimensional model proposes a new "C" (conducting activities). This function explains the intervention approaches in which counselors typically deliver services that address the needs of their clients but don't fall under the other three categories (for example, producing newsletters). Counseling and conducting activities are *direct* delivery systems; consultation and coordination are *indirect* interventions.

Program managers need to remember that these four C's are not always mutually exclusive. They may, at times, complement each other, and occasionally two or more delivery systems may be employed with the same client(s).

## Service Areas

The public needs to be told what services are provided so they can avail themselves of these services. Essentially, the service areas are those major services offered to the public for their use and for which clear-cut descriptions are developed to promote maximum appropriate use.

Follow-up, another function traditionally included under service areas, is absorbed by the evaluation component of the organizational model or is seen as an extension of a counseling intervention. It is not seen as a distinct service.

In summary, the Multidimensional Model for Counseling Program Management provides a conceptual framework from which one counselor or an entire program or agency may operate. It illustrates graphically how a system may be seen as a whole and how the parts are interrelated yet fairly distinct in their purpose and function.

All the service and delivery systems do not demand equal attention. The managerial situation that presents itself will dictate where proper emphasis should be placed.

Overlapping and duplication may occur, but the model minimizes these. Any overlapping or duplication that does occur may illustrate the complementary roles that such functions would play. More important, however, this type of model decreases the possibility that essential functions or services will be overlooked or omitted. Such a systematic look at the total program will promote comprehensive, efficient, and accountable programs.

## CAREER DEVELOPMENT

There are other models you may want to explore as well. One of these models, *career development*, illustrates how it can be infused into the paradigm we have just discussed. Because *career development* is really *life development*, schools that adopt this model stress the term *career* as a way of preparing students for life's major decisions.

The *National Career Development Guidelines* (National Occupational Information Coordinating Committee, 1989) provide a nationally validated model of career development that has been endorsed by most counseling organizations. The *Guidelines* also suggest that a comprehensive career development program focuses on self-knowledge, educational development, and career exploration and planning.

Career development is a concept that includes all of a person's life experiences that culminate in the development of a career identity. A model that is often promoted in our schools to foster career development has three stages: *awareness, exploration*, and *preparation*. Some models also include *placement* as the final stage, while others see placement as a part of preparation.

### Awareness

Small children are aware of the many different careers that contribute to their growth and their safety. Beginning with observations of people at work and continuing with concerns about how best to spend their allowances, students become gradually and developmentally aware that just about everyone contributes to a functioning world. An important function of the guidance program is to help students understand that paid and unpaid work both contribute to a better world. Often the contributions of homemakers, Peace Corps workers, and volunteers are overlooked in the study of careers—an omission the career component should correct.

Besides developing an awareness of the world of work, children also need to become aware of themselves. Self-awareness fosters the ability to make good decisions about the labor market based on knowledge of strengths, weaknesses, values, interests, and other factors.

The major notion at the awareness level is to expand the students' perspectives about the world of work and to promote an ongoing process of self-discovery. The awareness level lays the foundation for the exploration and preparation stages, but it does not stop when exploration begins. Developing self-awareness is a lifelong process.

## Exploration

The exploration stage of career development encourages students to make some tentative choices about areas of particular interest, and to investigate those choices more thoroughly before making commitments. Typical exploration activities include job shadowing, computer searches, employer interviews, and volunteering. This is also a time for exploring educational opportunities and choices related to personal, family, and social development. Individuals need to explore career opportunities that interest them. If these exploration opportunities happen at school, students will be more likely to understand the relationship between their academic programs and the world of work. However, career exploration should help individuals make informed choices about career directions. Although every student does not have to make a final choice of careers, most are encouraged to do so, and they are able to if they have developed a thorough awareness of self and the world of work and have carefully explored the options of greatest interest.

## Preparation

All in-school experiences, not just vocational programs, and out-of-school experiences, such as delivering papers, baby-sitting, and working in restaurants, are preparation for life/career. Many hobbies and sports activities provide valuable career lessons. Students need to be able to make the connection between their studies and/or their part-time work with their future life or career plans. High school counseling programs that spend disproportionate amounts of time on college admissions to the exclusion of preparation services for work-bound youth are not serving the preparation needs of a large group of students.

The typical counselor education program includes a course on career counseling/career development. You will have an opportunity to explore other models of career development in these courses.

## *ACTIVITY: LIFELINE* ⸻

On one side of an 8½ × 11 in. piece of paper, create a description of your life from the time you were born until today. You may use any technique you wish. Do not describe something that you are unwilling to share. When you have completed this lifeline, share your description with a classmate.

On the other side of the paper, create a description of your life from now until the time when you will be 100 years old—not an unreasonable expectation. Again, you may use any technique you wish, but do not describe something that you are unwilling to discuss. Share this description, also with a classmate.

How are you different from your partner? What are some common themes? Did you find any surprises about yourself? What other observations or questions do you have?

## *ACTIVITY: CREATING A MODEL*

Within your groups, discuss the strengths and weaknesses of the models presented thus far. Using the best of these, plus others that you may have read about in your texts, create a model for your group. Don't worry if some of the elements fit nicely into the scheme of your model while others may blend or cut across lines. Career development, for example, probably fits just about anywhere in the graphic. Crisis intervention appears, at first glance, to fit into responsive services; however, depending upon how the crises present themselves, crisis intervention may also fit into the guidance curriculum (preventive model).

## SUMMARY

In this chapter, you have had an opportunity to examine several program models. Although other models are available, these are the ones that are most complementary to the comprehensive developmental model that you will be creating in this handbook.

## REFLECTIONS ON CHAPTER 3

**1.** What's Going on in Your Group? _____

_____

_____

_____

_____

_____

**2.** What Models Are Favored by Your Group for Creating the Most Comprehensive and Developmental School Guidance and Counseling Program? _____

_____

_____

_____

_____

_____

**3.** How Do You Feel about the Progress of Your Group? _____

_____

_____

_____

_____

_____

**4.** How Do You Feel about Your Role in Your Group? _____

_____

_____

_____

_____

_____

**5.** What Questions Do You Have for Yourself, Your Group Members, or Your Instructor? _____

_____

_____

_____

_____

_____

**6.** Notes _____

_____

_____

_____

# CHAPTER 4

# Determining Program Priorities and Focus

In *Alice in Wonderland*, the Cheshire cat said, "If you don't know where you're going, you'll end up somewhere else." Not only do the guidance department members need to know their program priorities; the other members of the school and community need to know them also. In this chapter, we explain the procedures we believe will help determine your program priorities and assist you in informing the rest of the school and community about your program.

## NEEDS ASSESSMENT

We believe it is imperative that a comprehensive needs assessment be conducted before you begin to set or to change priorities. When you conduct a needs assessment, you must remember that you are not relinquishing control of your program. You are merely asking for input. There is no way that you can ever honor the requests of everyone who states an opinion about what topics need to be addressed. Therefore, you must inform people about what the needs assessment will and will *not* do.

First, a needs assessment seeks opinions about the content of the program. If you are talking about what people's *needs* are, you should focus on the issues in their lives that are the most urgent. Once you start wandering off into questions about whether you should be doing individual or group counseling, consultation, classroom guidance, or whatever, you are getting away from determining needs and instead are asking people to tell you how you should be managing your programs. True, it never hurts to get a little advice on such matters, but that's not the purpose of a needs assessment. Be careful about mixing apples and oranges. It should be easy to determine which topics demand the most attention in your program by maintaining a focus on what people believe to be their needs.

Make it clear that you cannot deliver services to meet all the needs identified. The needs assessment helps determine the *priority* services of your program while also determining which needs will have to be handled by some other program.

We also should explain that needs assessments are but one piece, albeit a major piece, of a complex method of arriving at program priorities. Our own knowledge and training must figure on the decisions also. We are the only professionals in the schools who have been trained to develop comprehensive guidance and counseling programs; therefore, we have the greatest expertise in the complexities and intricacies of a well-functioning program. We must bring that global understanding to any analysis of program priorities. At the same time, however, we must be wary of letting our biases and expert vision of guidance get in the way of seeing a different (and possibly better) perspective. Professional objectivity is the critical balance as we assert a leadership role in this process.

## TIME AND TASK ANALYSIS

Concurrent with the needs assessment, a guidance staff should conduct a thorough time and task analysis, an instrument used by counselors to survey and analyze the distribution of their time and the tasks that they are performing. Sample time and task analysis forms are included in many textbooks (Gysbers & Henderson, 1988; Myrick, 1987). It is important to have this time and task analysis completed and ready to use along with your needs assessment results when you meet with your planning committee (students will need to estimate figures). We suggest that the time and task analysis cover your guidance and counseling program tasks, guidance curriculum, individual planning, responsive services, and system support or program management. In addition, you should factor in the time that is spent on non-guidance functions. This information will be very important when you present to your school board what your community tells you needs to be done. If you can demonstrate that you are performing certain functions that could be more economically or more appropriately done by others, you will then be able to spend your time and your energy on programs your community tells you they need.

## ONGOING EVALUATION

Another piece of the priority-setting process evolves from an ongoing evaluation of the guidance program. Each year, as you assess the effectiveness of the programs and services you have delivered, you will receive feedback that can help you improve. Sometimes you may even receive information that suggests eliminating one of your projects. Letting go of familiar turf is one of the more difficult challenges for many counselors but at times it needs to be done. All feedback from a program evaluation must be combined with the needs assessment results to establish or change priorities.

## SOCIOLOGICAL ASSESSMENT

A final ingredient in the recipe for priority setting is a sociological assessment of the community. Each community has a unique personality and its own set of particular characteristics and issues. A community's ethnic heritage or economic circumstances, for instance, may impose certain pressures or influences on the students in its schools. Students in a town with a high dropout rate will probably not rate dropout prevention as a high priority; here, counselors should be the critical balance in evaluating this problem for the community.

## CREATING THE NEEDS ASSESSMENT

As with any kind of assessment, you should be concerned primarily with the content validity of your needs assessment. Listing all of your favorite counseling tasks or group counseling topics does not create a valid needs assessment. The more you rely on the professional literature to guide your choices, the more validity you should be able to expect from your instrument.

Figure 4.1 provides an example of a needs assessment that lists several topics for a high school guidance and counseling program. Note that blank spaces are left for people to add their own topics. The weighted priorities make it possible for certain topics to be identified both by the number of times they are cited, as well as by the relative importance they hold for those who are listing them.

By differentiating the responses of parents, teachers, students, and community members, the counseling program is able to discern whether various groups see similar priority needs or whether different perspectives will need to be addressed in program planning. This particular needs assessment was used in one school where students were also asked to identify their grade level at the top of the page. An interesting finding was that suicide was a major issue in the eleventh grade, but barely made anyone's list in the twelfth grade. Such a finding caused the counselors and administrators to take a more careful look at the reasons why. Also, the finding helped them know where to focus their attention (certainly during the junior year, but before then, as well).

## *ACTIVITY: IDENTIFYING NEEDS*

**1.** Using Figure 4.1, "Guidance Program Needs Assessment," complete the needs assessment according to the directions that are given.

    **a.** Tabulate the results for your group.
    **b.** Identify the priority needs, starting with the most important need area, then listing them in descending order.
    **c.** Discuss the findings.

**FIGURE 4.1** Guidance program needs assessment

SOURCE: Developed by University of Southern Maine students, summer 1991

The counselors would like your help in planning the guidance program. Please read the directions and give your honest feedback. Do *not* sign this form; just circle whether you are a student, parent, teacher, or community member. Thank you for your cooperation.

Student      Parent      Teacher      Community Member

I. The following list names some topics that might be addressed in a guidance program. Even though all these topics may sound interesting or valuable, we are trying to find out what students, parents, teachers, and community members consider to be the *most* important topics. We would like you to rank order the 10 topics that you feel would be most valuable in terms of your own needs or the needs of the whole school. Put the number *10* next to the topic that you feel would be most valuable, the number *9* by the next most valuable, and so on down to number *1*. Do not list more than 10. If you have some suggestions that are not included on the list, place them in the spaces that have been provided and include your suggestions in your top 10 rankings.

1. _____ Help with educational planning, curriculum, graduation requirements, and choosing courses
2. _____ Self-awareness and self-concept
3. _____ Life planning (Balancing occupation, family, leisure, and so on)
4. _____ Help for special learning needs
5. _____ Communication skills
6. _____ How other people influence our values and decisions
7. _____ Substance abuse
8. _____ Resolving conflicts and making compromises
9. _____ Problem solving
10. _____ Coping with difficult situations (Divorce, loss, moving, new school adjustment)
11. _____ Suicide
12. _____ Job-seeking and job-keeping skills
13. _____ Study skills
14. _____ Decision-making skills
15. _____ Help for transfer students
16. _____ Special enrichment programs (Boys'/Girls' State, Talent Search, Upward Bound)
17. _____ Orientation to guidance services and how to use them
18. _____ Exploration of personal goals and aspirations
19. _____ Help with postsecondary options, admissions applications, recommendations, and financial aid
20. _____ Dating/relationship issues
21. _____ Family relationships
22. _____ Peer relationships
23. _____ Social adjustment (Making friends, getting along with people)
24. _____ School/classroom behavior
25. _____ Sexual issues
26. _____ Physical or sexual abuse or neglect concerns
27. _____ _____
28. _____ _____

To determine program priorities, tally the items. Identify the items that have more 10s, 9s, 8s, and so on. Determine the final priorities by group consensus.

II. **Guidance services.** Typically, guidance topics are addressed through the six major service areas listed below with samples of the services. After reading the list, circle the appropriate number to rate the service areas according to the emphasis they should receive in the total guidance program.

| 4 | 3 | 2 | 1 |
|---|---|---|---|
| Top priority | Moderate priority | Fairly low priority | Very low priority |

4 3 2 1   1. COUNSELING SERVICE (individual and group counseling, support groups, referral to agencies)

4 3 2 1   2. TESTING SERVICE (achievement tests, career interest inventories, special needs assessment, personality inventories)

4 3 2 1   3. INFORMATION SERVICE (student records, handbooks, computerized data programs, postsecondary catalogues)

4 3 2 1   4. PLACEMENT SERVICES (enrichment programs, college admissions, course selection, career advising, referral to agencies)

4 3 2 1   5. CONSULTATION SERVICE (conferences with parents, teachers, and administrators; student assistance program)

4 3 2 1   6. CURRICULAR SERVICES (organization of materials for classroom teacher adoption, group and classroom presentation of guidance topics)

**2.** Explore what changes would be needed to make the needs assessment applicable to a middle school or elementary school setting.

**a.** Suggest changes you would make to improve the needs assessment in Figure 4.1, keeping in mind the cautions noted earlier in this chapter.

**b.** Generate needs assessment results that will allow your planning group to view your district's needs from a K–12 perspective.

**3.** For those who are creating fictitious results for the sake of expediting the planning process, this is also a good time to name and describe your fictitious school district. Describe the type of community, how many schools are in the district, how many students are enrolled, the number of school counselors, and so on (it is ok to be idealistic). Agreeing on this information may make the planning task more focused. For those who are using actual results from real school districts, it is still important to identify the demographic information to put all planning in perspective.

**4.** Compare your list with other students in the class. Are your lists similar? Have someone in the class compile the results for the whole class. According to the compilation data, what are the priority needs of this group? Discuss the process and write your findings here. _____

_____

_____

_____

_____

Which of these would you use in your district? Which populations would you assess with which instruments? Do you need to change some of the items? Do you need to create your own needs assessment?

## *ACTIVITY: CREATING MEANINGFUL INFORMATION* _____

Imagine that you will be on the receiving end of a group of educators or school board members who will be hearing about the needs assessment results for the first time. If you were sitting in their place, how would you want the results to be presented in a meaningful (from our accountability definition) way? Use this perspective to create a succinct report that can be included in your comprehensive plan.

## AGREEING ON A PROGRAM MISSION STATEMENT

One of the first steps your planning committee will need to undertake is the development of a mission statement for your program. Your statement should be consistent with your school's mission statement. You will also want to examine others that have been developed by different school systems.

Essentially a mission statement describes the scope and depth of the program you will create by utilizing the resources to address the community's needs. Often a mission statement will include terms such as *developmental, comprehensive, K–12, inservice*, and *cooperative*.

## *ACTIVITY: DEVELOPING A MISSION STATEMENT* _____

Brainstorming is a recommended technique for developing this mission statement so that no one's ideas are left out. Eventually, your committee will need to prepare a mission statement that is succinct and understandable. Try to avoid current buzzwords that defy definition. However, in this beginning stage of your planning, try not to spend an inordinate amount of time on developing a mission statement. You may find as you learn more about your comprehensive plan that you may need to rewrite your mission statement.

## *ACTIVITY: WRITING PROGRAM GOALS* _____

To establish appropriate program goals, you will need to determine the differences among program outcomes, student outcomes, and counselor outcomes. The first step is to define these outcomes by completing the following statements:

**1.** A program outcome is _____

_____

_____

**2.** A student outcome is _____

_____

_____

**3.** A counselor outcome is _____

_____

_____

Brainstorm some outcomes that you believe will result from creating a comprehensive guidance and counseling program. Keep in mind the program priorities established through your needs assessment analysis. Once you have a list of 10 to 12 outcomes, label each one program (P), student (S), or counselor (C). An example: Each student will leave the formal school setting with a career plan (S).

This activity is very important, as it sets the stage for your entire program. If you have counselor outcomes, program outcomes, and student outcomes all defined in measurable terms, you will be able to explain the goals of your comprehensive guidance and counseling program to any and all of your constituents.

## REFLECTIONS ON CHAPTER 4

1. In the Needs Assessment Activity, Did Your Identified Needs Align with the Group's Identified Needs? If Yes, How Did You Feel about that? If No, What Important Lesson Did You Learn about Needs Assessments? _____

_____

_____

_____

_____

_____

_____

2. How Do You Feel about the Progress of Your Group? _____

_____

_____

_____

_____

_____

_____

3. How Do You Feel about Your Role in Your Group? _____

_____

_____

_____

_____

_____

_____

4. What Questions Do You Have for Yourself, Your Group Members, or Your Instructor? _____

_____

_____

_____

_____

_____

5. Notes _____

_____

_____

_____

_____

# CHAPTER **5**

# Assigning Responsibilities

Who does what? In the first four chapters of this handbook you have determined what needs to be done to accomplish a comprehensive, developmental school guidance and counseling program. As a team, you have completed a needs assessment and determined those elements within the program that take priority over others. In Chapter 6, you will describe the human and material resources available to you to make your program work.

If you have developed a time line that includes all the activities that need to be done, then you know you must include other people in the implementation. In Chapter 2, we described a collaborative approach to building an ideal guidance and counseling program. By empowering others, we create broad ownership of the program. We hope each person involved will challenge the status quo and give the program renewed energy. Involving people in developing the program will make them more committed to its implementation, and involving as many as possible will help to assure a broad base of support.

Be sure to include programs that are already being carried out in your school, such as peer helper or teacher-adviser programs. The personnel who are conducting existing successful programs are valuable resources to you.

Now it's time to assign tasks and responsibilities to personnel and organizations—responsibilities that will get the job done. If, as a guidance team, you have conducted a time and task analysis, you have determined the elements within your program that must be done by counselors and also the tasks that can be done by others. This is a critical point. As an example, someone needs to convene a committee meeting. Who is the best person to set up this meeting? The guidance director? The principal? The guidance department's secretary? Another example: The team has determined that an advisory committee should be assembled. Who should draft the letter that invites business, industry, and community leaders to join this committee? Who signs the letter?

## PREPARING TO DELIVER YOUR PROGRAM

Borders and Drury (1992), in an exhaustive study that synthesized 30 years of empirical work and professional statements, concluded:

> There is a general consensus among professionals concerning interventions that should be included in a comprehensive developmental school counseling program. . . . Both *direct* and *indirect* services are identified, and these are frequently categorized as *counseling* and *classroom guidance* (direct services), and *consultation* and *coordination* (indirect services). (pp. 490–491)

In Chapter 3, we introduced delivery systems including a new "C," conducting activities, which includes classroom guidance.

### Counseling

Counseling, as a method of intervention, relates to the process for helping "individuals toward overcoming obstacles to their personal growth, wherever these may be encountered, and toward achieving optimum development of their personal resources" (American Psychological Association, 1956, p. 253). A counselor needs to determine when counseling is appropriate and when another delivery system may satisfy a client's needs just as well.

Within the delivery system, counselors need to make personal and professional choices related to theoretical approaches, ethical issues, and the limitations of the counseling intervention. A major program management consideration centers on the extent to which small group or individual counseling will be utilized.

### Consultation

At times the counselor acts as an objective party, looking at a situation and suggesting developmental, preventive, remedial, and other helpful interventions without direct contact with the client whose needs are being addressed. Models of consultation exist to help counselors gain skills in this area. Meetings with teachers, parents, industrial managers, support personnel, and administrators often utilize the counselor's consultation skills.

## Coordination

The successful counselor needs to be able to identify those tasks that can be done by another person, agency, or alternative means, and then provide the structure and input that will promote this intervention without his or her direct involvement. For example, referral systems, the facilitation of research studies, and career education infusion strategies demonstrate how counselors must be involved in organizing or facilitating such interventions, but careful coordination makes it possible for other personnel to implement these tasks outside the counseling program.

A counselor with good coordination skills may, at times, also enjoy the challenge of coordinating a major event or activity. Career days and guest lecture series illustrate the way highly visible programs can reach many people through excellent coordination.

## Conducting Activities

Many program activities just do not fit into the conventional three C's; instead they fall under a broad category making up the fourth C: *conducting activities*. While such activities do require careful planning and coordination with the teacher, the actual delivery of activities does not necessarily require the counselor to be directly involved in conducting the activity.

Classroom guidance is one broad category of conducting activities that may or may not be done directly by the counselor, but it is most effectively done by the counselor and teacher working together. One example at the high school level is cooperation between the teacher and the counselor to help students with the essays and other forms they need to apply for college admission and/or to complete job applications. These skills could be taught in an English or social studies classroom; the completion of the essay would earn class credit and accomplish the students' goal of being prepared for their next career step. The counselor works with the teacher in preparing the lesson and may enter the classroom for a short period of time to present the concept; the teacher is the writing expert and needs to carry out the lesson in his or her own way.

Many public relations activities, such as writing news releases, fall under the category of conducting activities. Conducting orientation programs, leading group test interpretation sessions, training peer helpers, conducting financial aid nights, and similar programs also are classified under this rubric. Because the counselors are *actively* (or directly) involved with the clients in these activities, it is obvious that they are not consulting or coordinating. However, an indirect result of these activities may be an increased involvement of teachers and other school staff members in the counseling delivery system.

## *ACTIVITY: APPROPRIATE ORGANIZATIONAL TASKS* _____

Listed below are some tasks that must be done in an effective program. Beside each task, list the most appropriate person(s) or organization(s) to carry out this task. Please add some of your own tasks to this list.

- Scheduling   _____
- Organizing reception for parents for National School Counselors' Week   _____
- Producing newsletter   _____
- Writing weekly local newspaper article   _____
- Teaching classroom guidance lesson   _____
- Training crisis team   _____
- Administering achievement tests   _____
- Interpreting achievement tests   _____
- Leading pupil evaluation team   _____
- Arranging bulletin boards   _____
- _____   _____
- _____   _____
- _____   _____
- _____   _____

As a follow-up to this activity, review the list and the person or organization that you have identified as mainly responsible.

1. Which of these responsibilities do you see as traditional guidance and counseling tasks?
2. If you have delegated these to others, how will you, or should you, monitor them so that you know they are being accomplished?
3. Is this the best use of staff expertise?
4. Is it possible to attach budget line items to the various program activities?
5. What is your time frame for changing from service-oriented to program-oriented delivery?
6. What other questions do you need to ask?

Looking at the preceding roles and responsibilities, describe your feelings about sharing power and authority with other professionals within and outside the school.

## INSERVICE EDUCATION

Frequently you and your counseling staff will determine that professionals within your school need to become more knowledgeable about a topic or a specific challenge before you can assign them a specific responsibility. Time that is set aside for schoolwide inservice education may be an opportunity for counselors to contribute to the inservice education of the teachers. For example, the counselors may have attended a conference where they learned about different learning styles. The counselors may believe that classroom teachers would benefit from an inservice day that focuses on developing curriculum materials that address different learning styles based on new research and application. You may want to decide how your planning committee would set up an inservice training day so that teachers would attend and willingly participate. You need to set up the agenda for the day and decide how you would determine whether the teaching staff applied their new knowledge.

## *ACTIVITY: EXPLORING INSERVICE EDUCATION* ————————

In your group, explore the following questions related to inservice teacher/ professional education:

1. Who in the group has conducted an inservice education program?
2. What's the best inservice program in which you have partici- pated?
3. What makes a good inservice program?
4. What are the challenges to counselors conducting inservice programs?

## DEVELOPING A TIME LINE

If all these activities seem to be overwhelming, remember they don't have to be done all at once. It is important for everyone involved to understand what the procedures are and approximately when each step is expected to be completed. As much as possible, every member needs to be involved not only in planning the event but also in setting the time frames within which those events will take place. Figure 5.1 represents the time line that the New Hampshire Comprehensive Guidance and Counseling Program set for the first phase of its development.

Steering Committee Tasks for the First Year of
Pilot School Involvement in the
New Hampshire Comprehensive Guidance and Counseling Program

Getting organized:

| Select steering committee members; assign work groups for conducting time and task analysis; write mission statement; coordinate needs assessment; etc. | Conduct time and task analysis | Involve administrators | Involve teachers | Create needs assessment instruments and conduct needs assessment |
|---|---|---|---|---|
| September through mid-March | Sept./Oct. through end of year | Sept. and Oct. | Sept. and Oct. | October through mid-March |

| Analyze and plan for use of needs assessment; publicize results; plan objectives | Develop curriculum based on program objectives | Begin to establish Master Calendar | Eliminate non-guidance functions | Make the transition |
|---|---|---|---|---|
| Mid-March | Late May through summer | Late May through summer | April through summer | Late May through summer |

**FIGURE 5.1** Time line—Phase I: Development

## SUMMARY

In this chapter, we have introduced you to the importance of sharing responsibilities for delivering a comprehensive school guidance and counseling program. When this has been accomplished, you will have provided opportunities for counselors to be part of an integrated curriculum.

## REFLECTIONS ON CHAPTER 5

**1.** How Do You Feel about the Progress of Your Group? _____

_____

_____

_____

_____

**2.** How Do You Feel about Your Role in Your Group? _____

_____

_____

_____

_____

**3.** How Easy (or Difficult) Is It to Decide Which Tasks Require a Master's Degree in Counseling and Which Tasks Could Be Done by Someone Without that Degree?

_____

_____

_____

_____

**4.** What Is the Most Important Thing You Have Learned about Assigning Responsibility Within the School Counseling Program? _____

_____

_____

_____

_____

**5.** What Questions Do You Have for Yourself, Your Group Members, or Your Instructor? _____

_____

_____

_____

_____

**6.** Notes _____

_____

_____

_____

_____

_____

_____

_____

# CHAPTER 6

# Organizing Program Support

You can have the best plan in the world and it will sit on the shelf, unused and unappreciated, if you don't have the support of all the human and material resources needed to get the job done. In this chapter, we will explain some of these critical support systems.

## PROGRAM POLICY STATEMENTS

To be an advocate for your program, you need to gather substantive policy statements that can lend clout to your arguments for a strong, comprehensive school guidance program. By using carefully selected quotations from legislative mandates, endorsements from professional organizations, or local school and district policies, you can add credibility to your planning efforts and gain important support.

## *ACTIVITY: IDENTIFYING POLICY SUPPORT* —————————

Before you begin this activity, you may want to refer to Appendix D: *ASCA Position Statement: The School Counselor and Developmental Guidance* or Appendix E: *ASCA Ethical Standards for School Counselors.*

1. Poll the members of your cooperative learning group to see which people have access to local administrative offices, which would be willing to contact local legislators, and which ones belong to professional education associations. Make sure each member of

your group takes responsibility for communicating with one of these groups.

2. Each person is then given a homework assignment to search for written policy or endorsement statements that support the development of comprehensive developmental school guidance and counseling programs. Included could be statements supporting broad initiatives that address more global issues, such as programs to foster positive self-image.

3. Each person is responsible for finding direct quotations that can be shared with your group. The shorter and more concise they are, the more they will be read and understood.

4. Describe as a team whether certain quotations will be used in the presentation of your plan.

## ADMINISTRATIVE SUPPORT

Without administrative support, it is unlikely that your program will flourish. The best possible scenario is to involve both the principals and the superintendent in the training process. One way to accomplish this involvement is to create a registration form for the training procedures that includes their signed endorsements. An even better way is to ensure their attendance at the training sessions by securing the endorsements of the state principals and superintendents associations. When administrators take part in shaping the program, they will remain involved in developing the change process that moves the guidance offerings from a service-oriented, reactive procedure to a program-oriented, proactive program. They will see that guidance has a program design and a budget similar to that of the traditional disciplines, and they will help open the communications door to the community and the school board.

## THE STEERING OR ADVISORY COMMITTEE

Once your plan has been developed, you may want to enlist the support of some key people who can assist you with the important decision making and public understanding about program priorities. In some places, this planning committee is referred to as a steering committee; in others, it is called an advisory committee. Either way, this is a working committee that assumes important responsibilities in overseeing the guidance and counseling program.

Committee members should not be volunteers. The group is too important to the program for its composition to be left to chance. Choose committee members carefully, considering the perspectives and responsibilities you want each to bring to the group's makeup. The committee should be representative of different community constituencies; nonetheless, it should be as small and as manageable as possible. We won't tell you whom you should have on your advisory committee, except for one person: an administrator. An informed, supportive, and well-respected administrator can provide tremendous leverage for promoting change and for enlisting cooperation. An administrator with K–12 responsibility can be very effective in helping counselors and those who are not counselors to maintain a K–12 perspective and to see the community implications for the committee's actions.

Some districts choose to use the planning committee that created their guidance plan as their advisory or steering committee. Others will use one group of proven veterans as their planning team, then open up membership to the steering committee to new members who have expressed an interest in being more involved.

In convening the first meeting of the planning committee (and probably each succeeding meeting as well, except in unusual circumstances), the head counselor (director of guidance) should take an active leadership role. This means that the counselor should generate meeting announcements and agendas, facilitate the meetings, and be responsible for all written materials that flow out of the meetings. The counselor may choose to include the guidance secretary for taking minutes or to delegate responsibilities after the first meeting; that would make excellent use of personnel. Try to limit meetings to one hour. If you have short meetings with tight agendas, and every member leaves the meeting with a task to complete and report on at the next meeting, you should have excellent attendance.

Most people do not want to come to a meeting and listen to someone talk about a program or to rubber stamp something that has already been completed. Well before the first meeting you should generate a list of items you would like planning committee members to do. You may want to distribute this list during the first meeting so that people have a sense of purpose and role expectations are clear. The list may include some of the following:

1. Review printed materials about the guidance program.
2. Discuss feedback from needs assessments.
3. Communicate information about guidance program priorities and services to other members of the community.
4. Present the perspective of the group you represent.
5. Participate in National School Counseling Week activities.
6. Offer suggestions and advice about program offerings.
7. _____
8. _____
9. _____
10. _____
11. _____
12. _____

The list is not exhaustive by any means. It merely shows the types of assignments that can be given to advisory, steering, or planning committee members so they see the important roles they can play.

The job of managing the counseling and guidance program ultimately falls on the shoulders of the counselor(s). You should not relinquish that responsibility to anyone else. You should always be open to (but not necessarily accepting of) any assistance that is offered. More important, however, you should feel confident that you have the knowledge and skills to use the information you have gathered to establish appropriate priorities for your programs, and then to create accountable programs.

## IDENTIFYING RESOURCES

Before beginning to change your guidance program, you should assess what already exists. Following are some examples of questions that you might ask:

1. What courses, programs, or teachers are already teaching the desired student competencies? How successful are they? Are the students learning the competencies? To what degree?
2. What additional human and material resources are needed for students to attain the desired competencies? Are the members of the community willing to allow students to "shadow" workers in their businesses or industries? Are there enough *Occupational Outlook Handbooks* in the guidance area or the library? Are the computerized college and career-finding programs up-to-date?

*Identify the Resources*
*You Have*

*Identify the Resources*
*You Need*

_____     _____

_____     _____

_____     _____

_____     _____

## DEVELOPING YOUR BUDGET

You must establish an adequate budget that reflects the resource needs of the guidance department. Most important, the school counseling program budget needs to be separate from the testing budget; counselors should also be separated from the duty of coordinating testing. As guidance and counseling in your district becomes an established program, your budget will take its place in the annual planning, like other school programs.

## *ACTIVITY: DESIGNING THE BUDGET* _____

In your group, design a budget. Exclude salaries, fringe benefits, and school-wide testing; these items are negotiated outside the guidance area. Your budget should reflect the resources you need to provide a comprehensive guidance and counseling program to all the students in your district. One method might be to organize the budget to match the basic components of your program: guidance curriculum, individual planning, responsive services, and system support. We have started your list; see how many more entries you can add.

### Guidance Curriculum
| | |
|---|---|
| Film Rentals | $500.00 |
| Primary Grade Curriculum/Training | $400.00 |
| AIDS Education Program | $1,000.00 |

_____

_____

_____

### Individual Planning
| | |
|---|---|
| Career Information System | $2,000.00 |
| College Information System | $1,000.00 |

_____

_____

_____

### Responsive Services
| | |
|---|---|
| Inservice Training: How to Work with Parents | $300.00 |

_____

_____

### System Support
| | |
|---|---|
| Postage and Mailing for Needs Assessment/Newsletter | $400.00 |

_____

Remember to include staff development funds to allow members of the counseling staff to keep their own competencies current.

## GRANT WRITING

Writing grants has become a way of life for some guidance and counseling programs. Many entitlement grants exist for schools to augment existing programs. Examples of entitlement grants are (1) the Drug-free Schools Program, for which each school/district must complete an application process, and (2) programs for special needs students. Generally, there are strict guidelines which the school must follow, such as providing in-kind funding or space, or promising to continue the project after the funding runs out. Also, grants are offered for very specific purposes. Donors almost never simply hand out money for the recipients to use as they choose.

To establish and maintain "grantspersonship" at any level, one individual should be designated as directly responsible for obtaining the grant information and, once the grant has been won, for carrying out the procedures within the grant. Some systems have office personnel whose only purpose is researching, writing applications for, and monitoring grants. Other systems rely on professionals within the different disciplines to determine the importance of a grant and then to write the proposal and carry out the grant, if awarded.

Include in your grant-writing efforts small special funding requests that involve local, regional, and special projects. Often local community groups and service organizations are looking for opportunities to invest time, funds, and energy into the student population. Projects that cost as little as $50 or $100 can provide your program with needed resources and create positive linkages with your community.

Before you request funding, you must decide how you are going to use the funds. Then you probably need to match your purpose to the person or organization from whom you are requesting the funding. For example, your school library may need an updated set of occupational outlook materials. You might consider writing a request to a local employer or to the regional office of the Department of Employment Security (DES). Where else might you look?

## ACTIVITY: IDENTIFYING FUNDING SOURCES

To identify possible grant sources remember where you identified some gaps in resource materials. Brainstorm some needs, possible sources, and methods for contacting the sources. We have given you a couple of examples just to get you started.

| Need | Possible Source | Approach |
|---|---|---|
| 1. Occupational Outlook Materials | DES | Letter/Phone |
| 2. Computer Software Program | Local Bank | Personal Contact |
| 3. | | |
| 4. | | |
| 5. | | |
| 6. | | |
| 7. | | |
| 8. | | |
| 9. | | |

In addition to these sources, you might consider using references that are directly targeted for proposal writing. Two that we have identified are *Getting*

*Funded: A Complete Guide to Proposal Writing* (Hall, 1988) and *How to Fund Career Guidance Programs* (Durgin & Drier, 1991). These and other sources indicate that you don't have to be an expert grantwriter to win grants.

Both authors of this handbook have written and received funding for a number of grants—some for as little as $200 and others as large as $100,000. The key to receiving grant money is to follow the guidelines printed in the request for proposal—the document from the funding source that announces the grant's availability and specifies the requirements for those seeking to qualify for the funds. Also, you need to ask yourself, "Do I have the expertise not only to write the grant but also to follow through with the implementation if I win the funding?"

Once you have read the grant application thoroughly and have determined that you will write it,

1. write clearly and specifically; don't use jargon
2. be sure there is a logical theme running throughout your proposal and that all parts of the proposal relate directly to the grant's purpose
3. don't apply for grants in fields where you have no expertise
4. give equal attention to each section of the narrative part of the proposal
5. keep the proposal within the specified number of pages
6. write out a budget page explanation showing the categories you would use and the amount to be allocated to each
7. write objectives at the task level
8. write objectives in measurable terms
9. review the guidelines to ensure that your proposal satisfies all of them
10. be sure to follow the mailing instructions

Once you have written your proposal, ask one or two people who have not been involved in the writing to critique it. Be sure to give them the proposal criteria. Ask them to pretend they are sitting in a windowless room at the U.S. Department of Education in Washington, D.C., and this is the fiftieth proposal they have read. Take their critique seriously, make those changes, then send your grant application in. And, good luck.

## REFLECTIONS ON CHAPTER 6

1. Of All the People with Whom You Must Work to Garner Support for Your Program, Which One Presents the Greatest Challenge? _____ Why? _____

_____

_____

_____

_____

2. What Can You Do about It? _____

_____

_____

_____

_____

3. How Do You Feel about the Progress of Your Group? _____

_____

_____

_____

_____

4. How Do You Feel about Your Role in Your Group? _____

_____

_____

_____

_____

5. What Questions Do You Have for Yourself, Your Group Members, or Your Instructor? _____

_____

_____

_____

_____

6. Notes _____

_____

_____

_____

_____

_____

_____

# CHAPTER 7

# Developing Public Relations Strategies

In Chapter 1, we mentioned that public relations (PR) was such an important topic that we were going to devote an entire chapter to it. However, we are convinced that even a whole chapter will not do justice to the significance of this aspect of your program. The image of school counseling programs and the image of the profession itself is dependent on the public's perception of what we do and whether we appear to be successful in doing it. The responsibility for building and maintaining the image of the profession of counseling rests as much with the individual counselor as it does with the professional organizations. No matter how you feel about it, you *will* have a public relations program, whether it is intentional or not. Intentional public relations just makes a lot more sense.

## CREATING AN INVITING ATMOSPHERE

You need to consider the influence of the media to appreciate the role that public relations plays in our lives. Can any of us say that we are not persuaded, on occasion, to buy something because of how it is presented on television or the clever message describing it on the radio or in the newspaper? We are not suggesting that school counseling programs develop major campaigns just for the purpose of improving their image. A very pointed message from the public relations literature is that PR cannot disguise an inadequate program. We advocate a "truth in advertising" perspective that attempts to inform the public, accurately and thoroughly, about what they might realistically expect from the school counseling services.

## *ACTIVITY: THE MEDIUM IS THE MESSAGE* _____

**1.** In a small group, discuss the ways media influence you in making decisions in your daily lives. Areas for consideration might be

clothes buying

hobbies and toys

grocery shopping

health and medicine

political campaigns

sports and fitness

entertainment

service providers

Just in case members of your group maintain they are never influenced by the media, discuss how "the masses" are influenced by television, radio, and print media.

**2.** What are the implications for school counseling programs? Generate a list of these implications.

**3.** Develop a rationale for the public relations effort of your school counseling program.

Recently one of us was responsible for the development of the *School Counselor's Resource Kit*, an annual public relations effort of the American School Counselor Association (ASCA). The challenge of putting together such a resource is not unlike the challenge confronting each school counseling program: *What do we emphasize and what do we omit—and what's the best way to present ourselves?* We cannot dismiss such a major challenge with the promise that we will work on it if we find the time! We need a plan. Public relations strategies must be a major component of the overall management plan that we develop for our school counseling program.

## PUBLIC RELATIONS CATEGORIES

One of the insights gained from working on the *School Counselor's Resource Kit* was the importance of categorizing the various ways that counselors can be responsive to the need for public relations. There are so many things counselors can do related to public relations that if we gave you a cumulative list of all of the ideas we have gathered over the years, it might prove overwhelming. We want you to be excited about doing public relations, not overwhelmed! By putting various possibilities into six broad categories, the task seems to be more manageable and more integrated with the other tasks that counselors must do.

### Organizing Public Relations Strategies

For each of the categories below—accountability, professional services, professionalism, publicity, student activities and events, and visual displays—we have provided you with one or two examples of public relations strategies that typify that category. We want you to use the creativity and resourcefulness of your small groups to generate other possibilities—believing that if you come up with the ideas, you will have more ownership and motivation to use them. Don't feel limited by the space provided; add all the good ideas you can think of.

### *ACTIVITY: PUBLIC RELATIONS THROUGH ACCOUNTABILITY* __

Because of your own sense of commitment to the ideals of accountability, as described in Chapter 1, you determine which activities will be most responsive to the demands of those who use and evaluate your program.

1. Submit an annual report to the school board, demonstrating how well you have addressed the goals of your comprehensive plan.
2. Meet regularly with building administrators.
3. _____
4. _____
5. _____

## *ACTIVITY: PUBLIC RELATIONS THROUGH PROFESSIONAL SERVICES* _____

There are many opportunities both within the school and in the community to be involved in activities that contribute to human development. Your visibility, commitment, and expertise will almost always be appreciated. More important, the public will begin to see the linkages between the mission of the school counseling program and the goals and activities of various groups who have the students' best interests in mind.

1. Serve on the advisory committee of a local community service organization.
2. Be an adviser for a school club.
3. _____
4. _____
5. _____

## *ACTIVITY: PUBLIC RELATIONS THROUGH PROFESSIONALISM* ___

Professionalism is the ingredient that helps professional counselors take the basic foundation provided by their educational training and build on it, so that they continue to grow professionally and assume responsibility for promoting and maintaining the image of the profession (VanZandt, 1990).

1. Present a workshop at the state counseling conference.
2. Be a model of mental and physical wellness.
3. _____
4. _____
5. _____

## *ACTIVITY: PUBLIC RELATIONS THROUGH PUBLICITY* _____

Communicating through the media can help to inform, educate, and enlighten the public. The messages and images that are created through the media can have a lasting effect on the public's perceptions of our school counseling programs.

1. Regularly send out a school counseling program newsletter.
2. Share program activities through the local cable TV station.

3. _____

4. _____

5. _____

## ACTIVITY: PUBLIC RELATIONS THROUGH STUDENT ACTIVITIES AND EVENTS

There are many special programs and group activities that may require some organization and coordination on the counselor's part, but the dividends are great in terms of students' levels of intensity and depth of involvement.

1. Celebrate National School Counseling Week (always the first week of February).
2. Develop a Step-Up Day for students who will be entering or leaving the school the following year.

3. _____

4. _____

5. _____

## ACTIVITY: PUBLIC RELATIONS THROUGH VISUAL DISPLAYS

By aesthetically displaying information and messages in conspicuous places, we can draw people's attention to key elements of our school counseling programs.

1. Develop attractive bulletin boards that focus on the themes from the guidance curriculum.
2. Wear lapel pins with counseling messages on them.

3. _____

4. _____

It is obvious from these activities that there are many opportunities to portray counselors and their programs in a more accurate and positive light. The possibilities for public relations activities are as extensive as the imaginations of those who take the time to generate a list of strategies. That is why public relations becomes an ideal way to involve your planning or advisory committee. Some advisory committees want to be involved in the actual implementation of the public relations initiatives; others would prefer to take part only in the brainstorming or decision making about public relations. Program leaders need to assess the committee members' level of commitment

to this task to determine their desired involvement and to delegate responsibilities.

## *ACTIVITY: PLAN OF ACTION* ────────────────────

As a final activity, we want you to create an annual public relations plan of
action (POA). From the numerous possibilities, we want your group to choose
at least one public relations initiative for each month of the school year.
(Taking on one per month seems to be more realistic than trying to do
everything on the lists that were generated—and will make you feel good
about your accomplishments.)

As you plan your activity, you should also plan to evaluate your progress;
make notes that will help you improve future efforts. In Figure 7.1, November
is filled in to illustrate this point. Complete the left hand column in Figure 7.1
for the remaining months.

**FIGURE 7.1**   Progress chart

| SEPTEMBER | |
|---|---|
| Activity | Progress<br><br>Comments |
| **OCTOBER** | |
| Activity | Progress<br><br>Comments |
| **NOVEMBER** | |
| Activity  Participate in Poster Contest and Poetry Contest as part  of National Career Development Month | Progress  Lots of participation in Poster Contest. Need to get Language Arts teachers excited about Poetry Contest.<br><br>Comments  Next year, meet with department  heads to generate enthusiasm. |

| DECEMBER | |
|---|---|
| Activity | Progress<br><br><br>Comments |

| JANUARY | |
|---|---|
| Activity | Progress<br><br><br>Comments |

| FEBRUARY | |
|---|---|
| Activity | Progress<br><br>Comments |

| MARCH | |
|---|---|
| Activity | Progress<br><br>Comments |

| APRIL | |
|---|---|
| Activity | Progress<br><br>Comments |

(continued)

| MAY | |
|---|---|
| Activity | Progress |
| | Comments |
| JUNE | |
| Activity | Progress |
| | Comments |

**FIGURE 7.1**   (continued)

After completing the plan of action, discuss in your group whether the plan satisfies all the goals you have set for your team in promoting an accurate and positive image. What changes might you consider?

As a final note, we want to remind you that public relations is a critical part of program support and a significant part of program management. As with other management tasks, we must set aside time to make sure those tasks receive the needed attention. It's a matter of establishing public relations as a priority.

## REFLECTIONS ON CHAPTER 7

**1.** How Do You Feel about the Progress of Your Group? _____

_____

_____

_____

_____

_____

_____

**2.** How Do You Feel about Your Role in Your Group? _____

_____

_____

_____

_____

_____

_____

**3.** What Is Your Level of Commitment to Public Relations in a Developmental School Counseling Program? _____

_____

_____

_____

_____

_____

_____

**4.** What Questions Do You Have for Yourself, Your Group Members, or Your Instructor? _____

_____

_____

_____

_____

_____

_____

**5.** Notes _____

_____

_____

_____

_____

_____

# CHAPTER **8**

# Establishing Program Leadership and Supervision

Just as there are styles of learning, there are styles of leadership. Each organization should utilize the leadership potential within all its members. Encouraging individuals in the organization to use their leadership skills for different tasks makes it possible to complete work that one designated or elected leader cannot. Often, the designated leader assumes all the responsibility for all the tasks and is not able to delegate work to colleagues. Or, a designated leader may choose to delegate all the tasks and not set a work example for colleagues.

## LEADERSHIP STYLES

There are great differences in leadership styles that should be understood and honored. We recognize, for example, that identifying the guidance program coordinator is a top priority. As program coordinators are identified (and perhaps information about their personality styles are shared), their leadership styles can be described. A great deal of time and energy can be saved if everyone understands and agrees to work with an identifiable leadership style.

## *ACTIVITY: IDENTIFYING LEADERSHIP STYLES* ⸻⸻⸻

Two people who have studied leadership styles are Hersey and Blanchard (1992), who identified leadership styles in four different domains or quadrants. If possible, before you go any further in this chapter, complete and score a leadership styles instrument, such as Hersey and Blanchard's *Leadership Effectiveness and Adaptability Description* (LEAD), or use the *Leadership*

*Styles* inventory in this chapter (Figure 8.1). Now ask yourself and your classmates these questions:

1. Do your results fit with your idea of your leadership style?
2. For what purposes and in what situations will your leadership style work best? Least well?
3. Is there a relationship between your leadership style and your personality type as described by the Myers-Briggs Type Indicator (MBTI) or another personality assessment?
4. Is this style congruent with your perception of a guidance counselor?

Develop a profile of the leadership styles of the class.

Next, create a matrix showing the relationship of the personality instrument and the *Leadership Style* results. What similarities do you perceive? What differences?

Just as there is no one appropriate personality type, there is no leadership style that is perfect for every challenge that a counselor meets in the everyday counseling situation. What is important is to be able to adapt your style to fit key situations within the work environment.

### *ACTIVITY: UTILIZING LEADERSHIP STYLE* _____

As you are working within your task groups for the balance of this class, try to identify the leadership style that is being used at any given moment. Stop every five minutes, or evaluate at times when you are stuck or when things are going smoothly. Try to do this consciously without interrupting the flow of your work.

### *ACTIVITY: MATCHING LEADERSHIP STYLES TO GROUP FUNCTIONS* _____

Refer to the group roles activity in Chapter 2, Figure 2.9. Review the role functions that you first identified for your group. Are they still the same or have they changed? For example, is the person who was the gatekeeper still performing that role? The person you have chosen as the director of guidance should facilitate this activity.

### *ACTIVITY: DEVELOPING JOB DESCRIPTIONS* _____

Before beginning this activity, you may want to refer to Appendix B: *Role Statement: The School Counselor*, and Appendix C: *School Counselor Competencies*. Using Figure 8.2, review the job description of the director of guid-

## FIGURE 8.1 Leadership styles

SOURCE: Developed by L. Painter and C. E. VanZandt, 1988, University of Southern Maine, Gorham.

Directions: For each item below, choose the letter of the response that most closely describes how you act in your role as supervisor. Base your choice on how you actually act, not how you think you should respond.

_____ 1. Rules and Regulations
   a. Insist that your subordinates follow the rules and regulations without exception.
   b. Allow your subordinates to do what they think is "right."
   c. Listen to your subordinates' explanation of exceptions to the rules and regulations and take these explanations into consideration.

_____ 2. Problem Solving
   a. Wait for your subordinates to discover the problem and find their own solutions.
   b. Solicit new ideas and solutions from your subordinates.
   c. Determine and implement new ideas and solutions as you deem appropriate.

_____ 3. Deadlines
   a. When approaching a deadline, require frequent updates from your subordinates.
   b. Allow your subordinates to complete their work as is convenient for them.
   c. Discuss the importance of meeting deadlines with your subordinates and solicit their cooperation.

_____ 4. Work Assignments
   a. Permit subordinates to decide their own work assignments without interference.
   b. Ask for volunteers for work assignments.
   c. Assume responsibility for assigning work tasks.

_____ 5. Interpersonal Relations
   a. Confine interactions with subordinates to work-related issues.
   b. Help your subordinates solve their personal problems.
   c. Avoid interactions with subordinates.

### Scoring

Directions: Circle the letter corresponding to your response for each item. Then, total the number of "1's", "2's", and "3's" circled.

|  | | | |
|---|---|---|---|
| _____ 1. | a = 1 | b = 3 | c = 2 |
| _____ 2. | a = 3 | b = 2 | c = 1 |
| _____ 3. | a = 1 | b = 3 | c = 2 |
| _____ 4. | a = 3 | b = 2 | c = 1 |
| _____ 5. | a = 1 | b = 2 | c = 3 |
| Totals | 1 | 2 | 3 |
| | _____ | _____ | _____ |

Lower scores indicate a more Autocratic style of leadership (5–7).
Average scores indicate a more Democratic style of leadership (8–12).
High scores indicate a more Laissez-faire style of leadership (13–15).

**FIGURE 8.2**   Job description

---

**Title:**   Director of Counseling and Guidance Programs

**Location:**   Clover School District

**Reports to:**   Superintendent of Schools

**Professional Qualifications:**   Master's degree in counseling from an accredited program; 3 years' experience as a school counselor, preferably with experience at elementary and secondary levels; qualifications for certification as a school counselor in this state; knowledge of services for accommodating the needs of all students; experience in the development, implementation, and evaluation of comprehensive guidance and counseling programs.

**Personal Qualifications:**   Has excellent verbal and written communication skills; shows evidence of leadership skills; is committed to program accountability and public relations; values team work; is committed to group and classroom guidance approaches; is flexible about time and work commitments; is highly motivated and enthusiastic.

**Job Functions:**   The individual filling this position shall be responsible for

1. developing, coordinating, implementing, and evaluating a written K–12 guidance plan based on the State Comprehensive Guidance and Counseling Program Model
2. directing guidance and counseling programs and services at the high school level to the following:
   a. vocational students
   b. students with exceptionalities
   c. students at risk
      Note: All other students will be assigned to other counselors in the school district
3. conducting regular public relations activities for the department at all levels
4. organizing and meeting with a K–12 guidance advisory committee at least three times annually
5. establishing linkages and networks among the high school, junior high school, and elementary school counselors, and community agencies providing services to the identified students
6. submitting an annual report to superiors highlighting program goals, accomplishments, future needs, suggested changes, and areas of concern

---

ance and counseling at Clover High School and (1) determine the leadership attributes in the job description, (2) determine which other desired attributes need to be added to the job description, and (3) rewrite the job description to reflect the kind of leader your group desires.

The director of guidance programs may be referred to under a number of titles. Figure 8.2 is a typical job description for the director of counseling and guidance programs in the Clover School District. Ideally, the person in this position has experience at both the elementary and secondary levels *and* has the authority to supervise the K–12 program.

## DEVELOPING MODELS OF SUPERVISION

The job description in Figure 8.2 is a perfect lead-in to our discussion of supervision. A good director of school counseling programs should be able to demonstrate competence in the areas of both leadership and supervision. Although the two entities are quite distinct, there is still some overlap that synergistically helps mold an excellent director of school counseling programs. A good leader will recognize and promote essential supervision practices. The good supervisor understands that effective leaders and role models may play significant parts in the professional development of a counselor. Furthermore, a good supervisor will nurture the leadership abilities of those he or she supervises, and a good leader will recognize that each counselor needs to develop to a point that he or she can eventually assume the role of supervisor. It is obvious that a reciprocal relationship and a developmental perspective provide a healthy framework in which both leadership and supervision can evolve.

Counselor supervisors typically play four major roles: counselor, consultant, evaluator, and educator. Simplistically, there are times when a supervisor may need to validate the feelings and needs of the counselor (supervisee), be able to discuss alternative interventions and facilitate decision making about a case, be able to assess areas of strength and weakness within the supervisee's skill repertoire, and be able to suggest educational resources and opportunities that fill in the gaps in a supervisee's training. There may be times when a supervisor will play all four roles within one supervision session.

A full discourse on the competencies that supervisors should possess is beyond the scope of this handbook. The purpose for exploring the topic here is quite different from the purpose of the American Counseling Association in endorsing 11 core areas of knowledge, skills, personal traits, and recommended training activities for supervisors (Dye & Borders, 1990). As a member of a school counseling team, you need to appreciate the importance of supervision for the overall efficient management of your program and for the development of your clinical counseling skills as you assist others with their developmental needs. Supervision is usually divided into the two broad categories of administrative supervision and clinical supervision, so it is important for school counselors to seek both kinds of supervision as they develop within the field.

A final note about supervision competencies: Competencies are usually divided into three broad categories—knowledge, skills, and traits. The knowledge and skills are fairly easy to assess. Your counselor training program has probably used tests, projects, and observation checklists to determine your ability to perform in many areas. Traits, however, are considerably more difficult to measure. For example, you might believe that a supervisor should be "sensitive." Most would agree that sensitivity is an admirable trait in a counselor and in a supervisor, but we would find it difficult to agree on one acceptable definition or on any observable indicators that objectify the concept of sensitivity. Many would also be concerned that counselors and supervisors could be too sensitive. Even though traits are subject to this dilemma of objectivity, the professionals who worked together to validate the supervision competencies through extensive research studies found that relationship factors were considered to be as important as technical skills in good supervision. One way to strengthen responses in this area was to clarify terms so that they have more specific relevance to the counseling field. Thus, instead of just using the term *sensitive*, one competency reads "is sensitive to individual differences," while another says "is sensitive to the counselor's personal and professional needs" (Supervision Interest Network, Association for Counselor Education and Supervision, 1990).

## *ACTIVITY: THE MODEL SUPERVISOR*

In your groups, explore the competencies of good supervisors through the following tasks:

1. On a chalkboard or flipchart, create three columns with the headings
   KNOWLEDGE        SKILLS        TRAITS
2. Have group members brainstorm competencies they believe a good counselor supervisor should possess. Have the group reach consensus regarding the column in which the competency should be placed.
3. Again, through consensus, identify the three competencies in each category that seem most important. Put an asterisk next to each of these.
4. Discuss the challenges of being a top-notch supervisor.

Just as careful training, skill development, and dedication are needed to shape the competence of supervisors, those who are supervised must also assume responsibility for extracting all they can from the supervision experience. Obviously, supervision is a process of communicating about skills, techniques, performance, and accountability. There must be two-way communication or supervision will be useless. Therefore, we all need to examine how we receive, process, and use feedback to affect our performance.

## *ACTIVITY: THE MODEL SUPERVISEE*

In your group, discuss the ideal supervisee.

1. What foundational knowledge and skills should a counselor bring to the supervision encounter?

2. What traits will assist the supervisee in taking full advantage of the opportunity of working with a person with more experience and training?
3. What should the supervisee look for in terms of program management supervision?
4. How can the supervisee assist the supervisor with clinical counseling supervision?

Program leadership and supervision may seem far removed from the critical issues confronting a school counseling and guidance program; however, that kind of thinking can spell trouble for everyone concerned. All counselors must see themselves as leaders. There are many ways to be a leader; it is just a matter of deciding how you will assert your leadership and how you will contribute to the overall goals and activities of the school counseling program. In some ways, supervision must concern all counselors, from the neophyte counselor just entering the profession to the venerable helpers who are now working with the grandchildren of their first clients. The profession is too complex and profound to allow any member to rest on the credentials of having received a master's degree in school counseling. In the developmental continuum, we should always be trying to improve ourselves.

## SUMMARY

A good supervisor is a leader; however, a leader is not necessarily a good supervisor. But any excellent school counseling program must have both good supervision and good leadership. Any time one member of the program's team fails to do his or her part in contributing to the whole in a well-run system, leaders and supervisors should recognize the problem and take steps to refocus the individual before the system breaks down. A chain is only as strong as its weakest link, and supervisors and leaders in a school counseling program should work diligently to assure that the weakest link is not weak at all.

## REFLECTIONS ON CHAPTER 8

**1.** What's Going on in Your Group? _____

_____

_____

_____

_____

_____

_____

**2.** How Do You Feel about the Progress of Your Group? _____

_____

_____

_____

_____

_____

_____

**3.** How Do You Feel about Your Role in Your Group? _____

_____

_____

_____

_____

_____

_____

**4.** What Questions Do You Have for Yourself, Your Group Members, or Your Instructor? _____

_____

_____

_____

_____

_____

_____

**5.** Notes _____

_____

_____

_____

_____

_____

_____

# CHAPTER 9

# Ensuring Personnel Development

Graduating from an approved counselor education program that leads to state certification in elementary and secondary school counseling is a beginning, a "commencement" in the counseling profession. Usually, this credential enables you to practice counseling in a public school. Some counselors believe that having attained this credential it is not necessary to keep learning. That is not the case. Fortunately, the counseling profession has many ways to keep counselors current and competent to work with today's changing school populations. In this chapter, we are assuming that you are a practicing school counselor and part of a team that is determining ( 1 ) the competencies that the team already has attained, ( 2 ) the competencies the team needs to attain, and ( 3 ) the strategies to attain these competencies. As you list them, remember to include the needs of other personnel with whom you work, such as clerical staff, paraprofessionals, peer helpers, and volunteers.

## *ACTIVITY: IDENTIFYING COMPETENCIES*

As a team, identify competencies that the counselors and other professionals in a comprehensive guidance and counseling program need to possess.

1. _____
2. _____
3. _____
4. _____
5. _____

**6.** _____

**7.** _____

**8.** _____

**9.** _____

What are some questions that the team needs to ask itself about these competencies? For example, does every member of the team need all of these competencies?

**1.** _____

**2.** _____

**3.** _____

Now, look at your list again and check those competencies that the team already has. The ones that are not checked provide the basis for your staff development training.

We have identified some methods of providing staff development or training below, to help counselors reach their maximum potential. Before scanning our list, please identify methods that you believe will contribute to your own and the team's competencies. We found nine. Good luck.

**1.** _____

**2.** _____

**3.** _____

**4.** _____

**5.** _____

**6.** _____

**7.** _____

**8.** _____

**9.** _____

**10.** _____

Here are the staff development methods that we determined could be used to enhance present counselor competencies.

1. **Individual group members:** Often, an individual within a team has an area of expertise that he or she can teach to others.
2. **Community agencies:** Resources such as mental health centers sometimes present staff development training workshops put on by experts in the field.
3. **Professionals:** Increasingly, professionals are packaging their expertise and offering staff development training workshops independent of an agency or organization.

4. Colleges and universities: Usually considered a traditional provider of courses and programs, most colleges also offer conferences and workshops intended to enhance the counselor's expertise.

   When an accredited institution changes its degree program, graduates of the program should return, if possible, and add any new, required courses to remain current.

5. Business and industry: Participating in pertinent workshops and seminars offered by business and industry provides not only training but also an opportunity for counselor interaction with the community.

6. Professional organizations: Membership in your professional organizations at the national level—the American Counseling Association (ACA) and the American School Counselor Association (ASCA)—and their state or local branches—will make available many professional development opportunities.

7. Government agencies: Local, state, and federal government agencies, such as your state Occupational Information Coordinating Committee, often sponsor training and development for specific programs.

8. Outside consultants: Sometimes a school district or a group within a school district identifies a need for some very specific training by a skilled trainer in that field.

9. Publishing articles: You will find that your own skills are enhanced as you attempt to explain and synthesize your ideas in a meaningful journal article.

10. Add yours here _____

_____

## ACTIVITY: STAFF DEVELOPMENT EXAMPLES _____

In your groups, list specific examples of some of the above-mentioned sources of staff development training. Try to list one for each source.

1. _____
2. _____
3. _____
4. _____
5. _____
6. _____
7. _____
8. _____
9. _____
10. _____

## BEYOND MEDIOCRITY

Many school guidance and counseling programs see minimum standards as maximum standards. You wouldn't want counselors serving your own children to possess such an attitude toward their job, would you? You need to think about how your school counseling program demonstrates that mediocrity is not the norm for your staff.

### *ACTIVITY: BEYOND MEDIOCRITY*

One of the major assignments in planning a comprehensive developmental school counseling program should be to synthesize your own thinking about the quality of the program you want to develop. This activity will probably take several weeks as you work through other activities and readings in this handbook. Your task is to write a paper that introduces the concept of exceeding minimum standards, then addresses five major aspects of quality programming and performance.

1. The profession's worth: Why do counselors play such an important role in today's schools?
2. Competence: Identify and explain the 10 most significant competencies you must possess to be an excellent counselor.
3. Image: Describe what contributes to the image of individual school counselors. What do you personally plan to do to create a positive image for yourself?
4. Professional involvement: Discuss the importance of being professionally involved. As a school counselor, what implications do your arguments have for your future personal/professional actions?
5. Excellence: What does an excellent guidance and counseling program do that makes it stand out from the other school programs?

After completing these five sections, write a summary that discusses what you have learned about yourself and/or school guidance programs as you have explored the various topics.

### *ACTIVITY: SELF-ASSESSMENT OF COUNSELOR INSERVICE TRAINING NEEDS*

Counselors need a variety of skills and competencies to implement a comprehensive guidance and counseling program. A self-assessment will help you identify your current inservice training needs and develop an individual plan to help you improve your comprehensive guidance and counseling program.

The form in Figure 9.1 is an adaptation of a survey originally developed by career and vocational counselors working with Belinda McCharen, State Guidance Coordinator, Oklahoma Department of Vocational and Technical Education in Stillwater, Oklahoma, and was intended to be administered to all practicing school counselors in the state of Oklahoma. The results were summarized, a profile was developed, and a mid-winter conference was planned to address the needs defined in this self-assessment.

**FIGURE 9.1**   Self-assessment of counselor inservice training needs

SOURCE: *Self-Assessment of Counselor Inservice Training Needs.* (1990). Belinda McCharen, State Guidance Coordinator, Oklahoma Department of Vocational and Technical Education, 1500 W. Seventh Avenue, Stillwater, OK 74074. Revised and reprinted with permission.

Read each of the following statements, and circle the number that best describes (1) how important this competency is to the implementation of a comprehensive school counseling program and (2) how high your need is to improve this competency.

| Importance | My Need |
|---|---|
| 4 = Very Important | 4 = Very High Need |
| 3 = Important | 3 = High Need |
| 2 = Slightly Important | 2 = Moderate Need |
| 1 = Not Important | 1 = Low Need |

After you have rated each of the statements according to its importance for implementing a comprehensive guidance program and your need to improve this competency, review the statements that you rated for both very important and very high need and select the five that represent your most important inservice training needs. List them in the "Most Important Professional Development Needs" at the end of the survey.

Thank you for taking the time to complete the form thoroughly.

**Counseling and Consultation**

1. Knowledge of general counseling and career development theories and techniques.

   Importance     My Need
   1  2  3  4     1  2  3  4

2. Knowledge of decision-making models.

   Importance     My Need
   1  2  3  4     1  2  3  4

3. Skills in building a productive relationship between counselor and client.

   Importance     My Need
   1  2  3  4     1  2  3  4

4. Skills in conducting group activities.

   Importance     My Need
   1  2  3  4     1  2  3  4

5. Skills in assisting students to deal with bias and stereotyping related to career decisions.

   Importance     My Need
   1  2  3  4     1  2  3  4

(continued)

# FIGURE 9.1 (continued)

6. Ability to help students identify and pursue postsecondary educational, training, and employment opportunities.

Importance      My Need<br>1 2 3 4      1 2 3 4

7. Ability to assist students in selecting courses.

Importance      My Need<br>1 2 3 4      1 2 3 4

8. Ability to assist students in the development of interpersonal skills.

Importance      My Need<br>1 2 3 4      1 2 3 4

9. Ability to assist students in matching developed academic skills with identified employment requirements.

Importance      My Need<br>1 2 3 4      1 2 3 4

10. Ability to assist students to interpret labor market information.

Importance      My Need<br>1 2 3 4      1 2 3 4

11. Ability to provide students skills to manage their lives.

Importance      My Need<br>1 2 3 4      1 2 3 4

## Information

12. Knowledge of the changing role of women and men and the linkage of work, family, and leisure.

Importance      My Need<br>1 2 3 4      1 2 3 4

13. Knowledge of strategies to store, retrieve, and disseminate career and occupational information.

Importance      My Need<br>1 2 3 4      1 2 3 4

14. Knowledge of educational trends and state and federal legislation.

Importance      My Need<br>1 2 3 4      1 2 3 4

15. Knowledge of state and local referral services/agencies.

Importance      My Need<br>1 2 3 4      1 2 3 4

## Individual and Group Assessment

16. Knowledge and application of assessment techniques, including measures of aptitudes, achievement, interest, values, and personality.

Importance      My Need<br>1 2 3 4      1 2 3 4

17. Ability to identify assessment resources appropriate to special populations.

Importance      My Need<br>1 2 3 4      1 2 3 4

18. Ability to identify assessment resources and techniques in terms of their validity, reliability, and relationships to race, sex, age, and ethnicity.

Importance       My Need
1  2  3  4        1  2  3  4

19. Ability to interpret and personalize assessment data.

Importance       My Need
1  2  3  4        1  2  3  4

## Management and Administration

20. Knowledge of program designs that can be used in the organization of guidance programs.

Importance       My Need
1  2  3  4        1  2  3  4

21. Knowledge of needs assessment techniques and practices.

Importance       My Need
1  2  3  4        1  2  3  4

22. Ability to assess the effectiveness of current programs and practices.

Importance       My Need
1  2  3  4        1  2  3  4

23. Knowledge of leadership styles.

Importance       My Need
1  2  3  4        1  2  3  4

24. Ability to identify/develop and use record-keeping methods.

Importance       My Need
1  2  3  4        1  2  3  4

25. Ability to prepare proposals, budgets, and time lines.

Importance       My Need
1  2  3  4        1  2  3  4

26. Ability to evaluate program and student outcomes.

Importance       My Need
1  2  3  4        1  2  3  4

27. Ability to convey program goals and achievements to key personnel in positions of authority: legislators, executives, and others.

Importance       My Need
1  2  3  4        1  2  3  4

28. Ability to provide data on the cost-effectiveness of counseling programs.

Importance       My Need
1  2  3  4        1  2  3  4

## Implementation

29. Ability to implement a public relations initiative for the guidance program.

Importance       My Need
1  2  3  4        1  2  3  4

30. Ability to manage a career resource center.

Importance       My Need
1  2  3  4        1  2  3  4

(continued)

**FIGURE 9.1**   (continued)

31. Ability to establish linkages with community-based organizations that provide placement services.

| Importance | My Need |
| --- | --- |
| 1   2   3   4 | 1   2   3   4 |

32. Knowledge of local and state employers as referral sources for employment opportunities.

| Importance | My Need |
| --- | --- |
| 1   2   3   4 | 1   2   3   4 |

**Special Populations**

33. Responsive to the unique issues and needs of minorities and other cultures.

| Importance | My Need |
| --- | --- |
| 1   2   3   4 | 1   2   3   4 |

34. Responsive to and knowledgeable of various handicapping conditions and necessary assistance and requirements.

| Importance | My Need |
| --- | --- |
| 1   2   3   4 | 1   2   3   4 |

35. Ability to identify community resources and establish linkages to assist students with special needs.

| Importance | My Need |
| --- | --- |
| 1   2   3   4 | 1   2   3   4 |

After you have rated each of the statements according to its importance for implementing a comprehensive guidance program and your need to improve this competency, review the statements that you rated for both very important and very high need and select the five that represent your most important inservice training needs. List them in the "Most Important Professional Development Needs" at the end of the survey.

Thank you for taking the time to complete the form thoroughly.

My Most Important Professional Development Needs

1. # _____ - _____

2. # _____ - _____

3. # _____ - _____

4. # _____ - _____

5. # _____ - _____

Name _____
(optional)

In your group, after each person has identified his or her most important professional development needs, try to reach consensus on the group's top three priority needs. What are the implications for future responsibilities related to professional development?

Remember that we have provided this survey as a guide only. Your program may need to develop its own assessment instrument for inservice training needs.

Continuing professional involvement makes it possible for counselors to grow and improve as practitioners. . . . Excellent resources and opportunities are provided for inservice training, individualized enrichment through reading and collegial support groups, requirements for continued credentialing, advanced degree programs, and other special services. It is professionalism, however, which motivates a counselor to take advantage of and to use the opportunities that are provided in these areas. Mandated, generic, staff development programs are not sufficient for counselors with professionalism; a personal plan of action is valued and pursued. (VanZandt, 1990, p. 244)

## REFLECTIONS ON CHAPTER 9

**1.** Have You Already Identified Specific Topics or Areas of Learning Where Your Counselor Training Program Did Not Provide the Level of Expertise to Allow You to Perform Competently and Ethically? What Are Those Areas or Topics? _____

_____

_____

_____

_____

**2.** How Do You Feel about the Progress of Your Group? _____

_____

_____

_____

_____

_____

**3.** How Do You Feel about Your Role in Your Group? _____

_____

_____

_____

_____

_____

**4.** Could You Identify Areas of Need for Some of Your Group Members? How Would You Approach the Task of Making Them Aware of Their Needs? _____

_____

_____

_____

_____

_____

**5.** What Questions Do You Have for Yourself, Your Group Members, or Your Instructor? _____

_____

_____

_____

_____

_____

**6.** Notes _____

_____

_____

_____

# CHAPTER 10

# Conducting Program Evaluation

The word *evaluation* often strikes terror in the hearts of graduate students, but most understand and appreciate the need to conduct evaluation continually and to use the results in applied research. You have completed some important applied research as you conducted the needs assessment in your school/district. The results yielded useful information for planning and developing your comprehensive guidance program. The needs assessment also gave you information about what is already being taught, and being learned, in your program, as well as information about what people perceived as needs that were not being addressed.

As you continue to develop and implement your program, ongoing summative evaluation is extremely important. Instruments need to be developed and applied to measure the extent to which the identified objectives are being met. It is not enough to say that the competencies are being taught; we need to provide reasonable proof that they are being learned in a useful manner by the students. Once the set objectives are measured or evaluated, you not only report on the level of attainment of these objectives, but you also set new or refined objectives based on these data.

## *ACTIVITY: EVALUATING YOUR PROGRAM*

Using the texts (Carr, Hayslip, & Randall, 1988; Gysbers & Henderson, 1988; Myrick, 1987) as references, design a survey instrument that will yield an evaluation of your entire guidance program. Your survey will likely be organized around the four program components: guidance curriculum, individual planning, responsive services, and system support. We suggest that you refer to your time and task analysis and your needs assessment documents (Chapter 4) to form the baseline for your survey. In addition to using your texts, you may want to refer to *Evaluating Guidance Programs: A Practitioner's Guide*

(Johnson & Whitfield, 1991) or an excellent article, "Improving School Guid-ance Programs: A Framework for Program, Personnel, and Results Evaluation" (Gysbers, Hughey, Starr, & Lapan, 1992).

Following are activities that address three very important issues in the evaluation of your comprehensive school guidance and counseling program. In three separate groups, complete one of the following activities and try out your evaluation on the other two groups. You will need to explain the evaluation procedure before involving the group members in the activity.

## *ACTIVITY: EVALUATING FINANCIAL RESOURCES* _____

In Chapter 6, you were asked to develop a guidance program budget. Now, look back at that budget and design an evaluation that will enable you to report to your school board that the funds are being appropriately spent. This can be a simple five- or six-question evaluation. An important aspect of this evaluation is that, with this information, you will be able to justify your budget and, perhaps, an increase for the following year.

## *ACTIVITY: SCHOOL COUNSELOR PERFORMANCE APPRAISAL* __

Too often the performance of school counselors is measured with the same checklist/instrument as that used for teachers. We contend that although the teaching role is embedded in much of what the counselor does, the separate responsibilities of the counselor require a different evaluation instrument. Rather than ask you to design one, we are including a sample high school counselor performance appraisal instrument, for you to modify if you wish (Figure 10.1).

## *ACTIVITY: STUDENT COMPETENCY EVALUATION* _____

To develop student competency evaluations, you need to refer to your needs assessment results in Chapter 4. Ask yourself these questions:

1. What competencies did the teachers, students, and community identify as priority needs?
2. Were these competencies covered either in the guidance curriculum or in another organized curriculum?
3. How will you know that the student(s) learned these competencies?

Finally, those who are being evaluated need to know what they are being evaluated for and how the results will be used. Also, evaluating the program elements as they are applied will enable you to make some fine-tuning changes during the school year. In the texts that are being used in your guidance courses, there are several additional recommended forms to use for evaluation purposes. We suggest you write your own based on these models.

**FIGURE 10.1**   Oxford Hills High School counselor performance
appraisal instrument

SOURCE: Developed by Kathryn VanZandt, Director of Guidance Programs, Oxford Hills High
School, South Paris, Maine

1. The counselor completes the performance appraisal instrument as a self-evaluation.
2. The counselor and evaluator meet to discuss the evaluation.
3. The evaluator rates the school counselor on the scale as indicated.
4. The evaluator is encouraged to add pertinent comments at the end of each major function.
5. The school counselor is provided an opportunity to react to the evaluator's ratings and comments.
6. The school counselor and the evaluator must sign the instrument in the assigned spaces.
7. The instrument must be filed in the school counselor's personnel file.

Counselor's Name _____   Date of Appraisal _____

Key: Column 1   Exceeds Expectations
Column 2   Meets Expectations
Column 3   Needs Improvement

A.  Major Function: Responsive Services
(Consultation, Counseling, and Referral)           1          2          3
   1. Provides individual school guidance and
      counseling for students to meet their
      remedial/academic, social, and/or
      developmental needs. [Indicators: In
      majority of cases, when students are
      referred by teachers, or self-refer,
      counselor meets with the student.]          _____   _____   _____
   2. Provides for group counseling for
      students to meet their remedial/academic,
      social, and/or developmental needs.
      [Indicators: (a) When students are
      referred, provides for group counseling,
      as resources permit. (b) Assesses and
      identifies students' needs for group
      counseling.]                                 _____   _____   _____
   3. Consults with school personnel, parents,
      and community agencies about the needs
      and concerns of students. [Indicators:
      (a) Within a reasonable time frame,
      counselor consults with others. (b) Calls
      and/or arranges meetings with parents
      when specific problems arise, such as
      emotional issues, family death.]             _____   _____   _____
   4. Makes appropriate referrals to agencies.
      [Indicators: (a) Refers students as
      appropriate and as resources permit.
      (b) Demonstrates awareness of
      referral sources.]                           _____   _____   _____

Comments: _____

(continued)

## FIGURE 10.1 (continued)

B.  Major Function: Planning and Advising
    (Educational and Career Planning; Student
    Assessment and Appraisal)                              1        2        3

    1. Provides information to students about
       career and life planning, including up-to-
       date career and higher education
       information, using Guidance Information
       System (GIS), other resources.                    _____   _____   _____

    2. Assists school personnel, parents, and
       students in evaluating, interpreting, and
       utilizing appraisal data for meeting
       student needs, such as Pupil Evaluation
       Team (PET), Student Assistance team.
       Examples: (a) Helps faculty, parents, and
       students understand the contents of
       cumulative records. (b) Gives summary
       of students' records at meetings. (c)
       Provides progress reports of students
       for parents.                                       _____   _____   _____

    3. Assists in coordinating testing programs
       [Maine Educational Assessment (MEA),
       Armed Services Vocational Aptitude
       Battery (ASVAB), Scholastic Aptitude
       Tests (SATs), and Preliminary Scholastic
       Aptitude Tests (PSATs)]                            _____   _____   _____

    4. Assists students in achieving successful
       educational and vocational placement
       based on aptitude, achievement, and
       interest.                                          _____   _____   _____

    5. Assists students in developing four-year
       plan and choosing appropriate courses to
       implement the plan.                                _____   _____   _____


Comments _____

_____


C.  Major Function: Group Guidance                         1        2        3

    1. Provides leadership in the development
       and implementation of appropriate group
       guidance activities (financial aid, human
       relations, employability skills,
       postsecondary educational opportunities).
       Examples: (a) Participates in schoolwide
       group guidance activities as planned by
       the department. (b) Leads or co-leads
       group guidance activities on specific
       topics.                                            _____   _____   _____

    2. Assists in providing orientation for
       students in order to help ensure
       successful school adjustment, as from
       one school to another, one grade level
       to another, new students.                          _____   _____   _____

3. Provides parents with information that helps meet the needs of students, (such as parenting/communication skills, financial aid, vocational opportunities, postsecondary planning). _____ _____ _____

Comments: _____

_____

D. Major Function: Professional Ethics, Growth, and Development       1     2     3
    1. Adheres to ethical standards of the counseling profession (follows the ethical code for counselors re: confidentiality, release of information, conflict of interest). _____ _____ _____
    2. Demonstrates positive human relations by showing respect for the worth and dignity of all students. _____ _____ _____
    3. Establishes and maintains cooperative relationships with other staff in the building. _____ _____ _____
    4. Serves as an appropriate role model for students. _____ _____ _____
    5. Is aware of, and values, cultural differences. _____ _____ _____
    6. Pursues personal and professional growth and development. _____ _____ _____
    7. Follows established procedures and regulations in the building. _____ _____ _____
    8. Adheres to federal and state laws pertaining to educational and employment placement (such as discrimination, child labor laws, new high school programs, makeup guidelines). _____ _____ _____

Comments: _____

_____

Evaluator's Summary Comments: _____

_____

_____

Counselor's Reactions to Evaluation: _____

_____

_____

_____    _____
Evaluator's Signature/Date             Counselor's Signature/Date

Signature of counselor acknowledges that the counselor has reviewed and has had an opportunity to discuss the evaluation; signature does not necessarily indicate agreement with the evaluation.

## REFLECTIONS ON CHAPTER 10

1. How Satisfied Are You with Your Group's Evolving Developmental School Guidance and Counseling Program? _____

_____

_____

_____

_____

2. How Do You Feel about Individual Group Members' Contributions? _____

_____

_____

_____

_____

3. What Evaluation Technique Would You Use to Assess Your Group's Process and Products? _____

_____

_____

_____

_____

4. How Do You Feel about Your Role in Your Group? _____

_____

_____

_____

_____

5. What Questions Do You Have for Yourself, Your Group Members, or Your Instructor? _____

_____

_____

_____

_____

6. Notes _____

_____

_____

_____

_____

_____

_____

# CHAPTER 11

# Synthesis

In Chapter 2, we challenged you to remain objective as you explored some of the facets of systems thinking. The entire handbook has asked you to see the Big Picture and then to analyze its component parts as you participated in the exercises in each chapter. Now it is important for you to put the pieces back together again. We are confident that what you see will look more complete now.

This chapter has three activities to help you synthesize the content of the entire handbook. By reexamining your group's original flowchart, making a school board presentation, and then reviewing the process that completes the facilitation of your group's task, you should be able to integrate the most essential elements of a comprehensive developmental school guidance and counseling program.

## *ACTIVITY: REVISITING THE FLOWCHART*

Take a few minutes to review the flowchart your group created in Chapter 2. Discuss the following questions:

1. Did you use the flowchart in setting the direction for your group's actions?
2. Has your flowchart evolved into a more refined product?
3. Did the flowchart help in accomplishing your group's tasks? If yes, why? If no, why not?
4. What are some differences in how various members of your group used flowcharting to conceptualize all or parts of the program?
5. Is there a place for a flowchart in your group's school board presentation?

## *ACTIVITY: THE SCHOOL BOARD PRESENTATION* _____

Now is the time for you to package your plan and sell it to the school board. To do this, we suggest you go back and review key messages from the previous chapters. For example, in Chapter 1, we asked you to reflect on what was "meaningful information." What information do you believe will be most meaningful to a school board?

Remember which roles you were to play with the planning groups. Try to represent those roles to the school board. How will you tap people's strengths and talents? You may want to videotape your presentation.

Consider how long a typical school board presentation lasts (for a major presentation, of course). Try to stay within that same time frame in making your presentation. How much can they take in? What do you want them to remember most about your presentation? What about the learning styles of school board members?

When one of the class groups is presenting its program model, the other class group acts as a school board. As you are playing the role of the school board member, you need to consider certain political possibilities. Pause for a moment and visualize what a school board member might be looking for in such a presentation. Try to think like the school board member. Help the members of the other group face some of the realities of making a school board presentation. Although the temptation will be great at times, try not to overdo the role-playing; just make it as real as possible.

After you have made your presentation, write down the following observations:

**1.** The best part of our group's presentation: _____

_____

_____

_____

**2.** An important question raised by the board: _____

_____

_____

_____

**3.** How I felt about my individual part in the presentation: _____

_____

_____

_____

**4.** Items in our plan that may need further attention: _____

_____

_____

_____

**5.** What I learned about making school board presentations: _____

_____

_____

_____

Upon further reflection about your final product, consider the following:

**1.** How successful have you been in visualizing an entire guidance and counseling program? _____

_____

_____

_____

**2.** How does your plan reflect systems thinking? _____

_____

_____

_____

**3.** What was the turning point or catalyst for your group to obtain and maintain a common focus? _____

_____

_____

_____

**4.** What are the special features of your plan? _____

_____

_____

_____

**5.** What did the other team have in its plan that you wish you had in yours? _____

_____

_____

_____

**6.** Being as objective as possible, how would you assess the technical and aesthetic quality of your final product? _____

_____

_____

_____

**7.** Add any other comments about your group's final plan. _____

_____

_____

_____

## *ACTIVITY: PROCESSING THE PROCESS* _____

One of the major strategies of the cooperative learning experience that was used to create your guidance plan has been to thrust you into a group process that is not unlike many you will encounter as a school counselor. Because you have been so involved in developing a *product*, you may not have been able to appreciate all the lessons that may be learned from the *process*. The outline below is designed to help you process the process:

1. Early in the semester, we mentioned that you would be moving through three—and possibly four—typical stages of group process (forming/storming/norming/performing). To what extent was this movement realized in your planning group?

    | 4 | 3 | 2 | 1 |
    |---|---|---|---|
    | Very much | To a considerable degree | Somewhat | Not at all |

2. To what degree did cooperative learning contribute to the quality of your final product?

    | 4 | 3 | 2 | 1 |
    |---|---|---|---|
    | Very much | To a considerable degree | Somewhat | Not at all |

3a. To what degree did you feel competition with the other groups?

    | 4 | 3 | 2 | 1 |
    |---|---|---|---|
    | Very much | To a considerable degree | Somewhat | Not at all |

3b. If you felt competition, what was the source of the feeling? _____

    _____

    _____

3c. If School District A and School District B are given the task of designing comprehensive guidance plans, how much should they cooperate in that mission?

4a. Each of you was assigned a role to represent within your planning group. Although assignment of such roles is artificial, you must recognize that in the real world people with even less vision about guidance and counseling will often fill these roles. How important was it for the planning group to keep the different role perspectives in mind in the development of your plan?

    | 4 | 3 | 2 | 1 |
    |---|---|---|---|
    | Very much | To a considerable degree | Somewhat | Not at all |

**4b.** What was the significance of having those roles in this group process? _____

_____

_____

_____

**4c.** How open were you to the perceptions of people as they represented their roles?

| 4 | 3 | 2 | 1 |
|---|---|---|---|
| Very much | To a considerable degree | Somewhat | Not at all |

**5.** What "group" lessons did you learn from this project that you feel will be applicable to your work as a school counselor? _____

_____

_____

_____

**6.** What "planning" lessons did you learn from this project that you feel will be applicable to your work as a school counselor? _____

_____

_____

_____

**7.** What things did you discover about yourself during this group experience? _____

_____

_____

_____

**8.** One of the major challenges given to you in the beginning of the course was to choose a director of guidance (a person and a position about which you knew very little). In reflecting on the last semester's experience, think about the implications for your future. What did you learn about leadership?

On a separate sheet of paper, provide some feedback to the leader of your group. Use the following outline:

**a.** Things you did well:

_____

_____

_____

**b.** Things I think you need to be aware of:

_____

_____

_____

c. A comment about our final product and the role you played in its development:

_____

_____

_____

9. On another piece of paper, write your name in bold letters at the top and circulate the paper so each of the other members of your group can write something positive or validating about your contribution to the group and its mission.
10. Please list any other lessons learned or comments that will help you remember the essential facets of this cooperative learning experience.

_____

_____

_____

## SUMMARY

You have worked diligently to produce a comprehensive, developmental school guidance and counseling program model of which your group can be proud and, more important, which empowers each of you to go out and do it the right way! We are fully aware that these exercises and activities have been demanding. We congratulate you on gaining important insights into the complexity and significance of team planning and focused programming.

# Sample Course Outline

## ORGANIZATION OF GUIDANCE PROGRAMS

### Course Description

Elements of a guidance counselor's work in a public school setting include (1) developing and implementing a comprehensive guidance and counseling program with emphasis on a balance of responsive services, systems support, individual planning, and guidance curriculum; (2) legal and ethical considerations; (3) class scheduling and placement; (4) research and follow-up; and (5) the curriculum development function.

### Course Goal

To introduce prospective school guidance counselors to a model for planning, developing, implementing, and evaluating a comprehensive guidance and counseling program with emphasis on student competencies.

### Course Objectives

To assist students to

1. become familiar with historical and social perspectives of guidance and counseling in the elementary and secondary schools (K–12)
2. understand goals, objectives, and philosophical tenets of guidance and counseling and their integration into the school curriculum
3. become familiar with the nature and influence of family, community, society, and culture on children, and how these topics may be integrated to enhance student learning

4. explore functions of school counseling in the following areas:
   **a.** individual and group counseling
   **b.** consultation
   **c.** liaison and public relations
   **d.** coordination
   **e.** career development
   **f.** curriculum
   **g.** professional growth and program development
   **h.** research and innovation
   **i.** accountability
   **j.** measurement and evaluation
   **k.** ethics and legal issues
5. develop and implement classroom guidance units and curriculum
6. develop and contribute to comprehensive developmental guidance and counseling programs

Required Text (one or more of the following):

Gysbers, N., & Henderson, P. (1988). *Developing and managing your school guidance program*. Alexandria, VA: American Association for Counseling and Development.
Carr, J., Hayslip, J., & Randall, J. (1988). *New Hampshire comprehensive guidance and counseling program: An approved model for program development.* Plymouth, NH: Plymouth State College.
Herlihy, B., & Golden, L. B. (1990). *Ethical standards casebook*. Alexandria, VA: American Association for Counseling and Development.
Myrick, R. D. (1993). *Developmental guidance and counseling: A practical approach*. Minneapolis, MN: Educational Media Corporation.

## Course Requirements

1. Attend and participate in all classes.
2. Goodie File: Obtain a file box, 5 × 8 in. index cards, and some tab labels to categorize information in the file box. During the course, organize and compile information in the file that you can use as a school counselor. One system will not work for everyone; therefore, develop your own system of categories and organization, but arrange it so that others will be able to use the system as well. Try to think of typical areas in your work setting you will need to refer to often for resources and ideas. Due on _____ .
3. Group Project—Guidance Plan: The class will be divided into two planning groups for the purpose of developing a comprehensive K–12 guidance plan. On the first day of class, you will be assigned roles and you will assume your same role on the committee throughout the course.

   Two of the most important tasks on the first day will be to identify your director of guidance (who will facilitate your team's work) and to select a scribe (one member of the team) who will compile the information from the team, keep minutes, and help provide any written or visual assistance (such as recording brainstorming ideas on chalkboards or flipcharts) so that the team can agree on the content of the sessions.

The guidance plan must include these elements:

a. Title page and committee representatives
b. Mission statement
c. Description of how program needs will be identified
d. Determination of student outcomes versus counselor outcomes
e. Framework of a model comprehensive guidance and counseling program
f. Time lines
g. Program evaluation
h. Budget

Grading will be based on the thoroughness of the plan, the quality of the content, and the technical presentation. Due date is the last night of class when each team will present its plan.

4. Guidance Unit: In pairs, prepare a curriculum unit based on a cluster of competencies described in the appendix of either the Gysbers or the Carr textbook. In not more than 30 minutes, present this curriculum to the class using at least one of the activities in the curriculum to involve the class members in the learning experience. The curriculum presented should be as original as possible, should fit the curriculum guidelines presented by the professor, and should be useful to the presenter in his or her present or future work setting.

Grading will be based on the practicality of the unit (its usefulness for the group for which it was designed), the quality of the content, and the technical quality of the product.

Prepare a one-page abstract of your unit that can be shared with the class. Classroom guidance units are due by the end of the twelfth week.

5. Beyond Mediocrity Paper: Write a paper that synthesizes some of your thinking about school guidance and counseling programs. The paper needs to include the following headings, after the obligatory introduction:

a. The Profession's Worth—Why do counselors play such an important role in today's schools?
b. Competence—What are the 10 most significant competencies you must possess to be an *excellent* school counselor?
c. Image—What contributes most to the image of individual school counselors? What do you personally plan to do to create a positive image for yourself?
d. Professional Involvement—Discuss the importance of being professionally involved as a school counselor. What implications

do your arguments have for your personal and professional actions?

**e.** Excellence—Many guidance and counseling programs see minimum standards as maximum standards. You wouldn't want counselors serving your own children to possess such an attitude toward their jobs, would you? What can your school guidance and counseling program do to demonstrate that mediocrity is not the norm for its guidance program? What does an excellent guidance program do that makes other guidance programs envious?

**f.** Summary—What have you learned about yourself and/or school guidance programs as you have explored this topic?

You may want to include graphs, resources, and other materials as you write this paper and as you later reflect on what you wrote and why you wrote it. The paper should be written according to the style guidelines of the American Psychological Association *Publication Manual*. Grading will be based on the substance of your ideas and arguments, the development of those ideas and arguments, and the technical quality of the paper (adherence to APA guidelines). The paper is due _____ .

## Grading for Course

| | |
|---|---|
| Class Participation | 10% |
| Goodie File | 15% |
| Classroom Guidance Unit | 20% |
| Beyond Mediocrity Paper | 25% |
| Guidance Plan | 30% |

Completion of the course requirements does not assure you of an A in the course. The quality of your work will determine the quality of your grade.

A grade of incomplete will be given only under extraordinary circumstances, such as illness, death in the family, or change in job responsibilities.

# ASCA Role Statement: The School Counselor

The American School Counselor Association recognizes and supports the implementation of comprehensive developmental counseling programs at all educational levels. The programs are designed to help all students develop their educational, social, career, and personal strengths and to become responsible and productive citizens. School counselors help create and organize these programs, as well as provide appropriate counselor interventions.

School counseling programs are developmental by design, focusing on needs, interests, and issues related to the various stages of student growth. There are objectives, activities, special services and expected outcomes, with an emphasis on helping students to learn more effectively and efficiently. There is a commitment to individual uniqueness and the maximum development of human potential. A counseling program is an integral part of a school's total educational program.

## THE SCHOOL COUNSELOR

The school counselor is a certified professional educator who assists students, teachers, parents, and administrators. Three generally recognized helping processes used by the counselor are counseling, consulting and coordinating: 1) Counseling is a complex helping process in which the counselor establishes a trusting and confidential working relationship. The focus is on problem-solving, decision-making, and discovering personal meaning related to learning and development; 2) Consultation is a cooperative process in which the

SOURCE: American School Counselor Association. (1990). *Role statement: The school counselor*. Alexandria, VA: Author. Reprinted with permission.

counselor-consultant assists others to think through problems and to develop skills that make them more effective in working with students; 3) Coordination is a leadership process in which the counselor helps organize and manage a school's counseling program and related services.

School counselors are employed in elementary, middle/junior high, senior high, and postsecondary schools. Their work is differentiated by attention to age-specific developmental stages of growth and related interests, tasks, and challenges. School counselors are human behavior and relationship specialists who organize their work around fundamental interventions.

Counselor interventions have sometimes been referred to as functions, services, approaches, tasks, activities, or jobs. They have, at times, been viewed as roles themselves, helping to create the image of the counselor. In a comprehensive developmental counseling program, school counselors organize their work schedules around the following basic interventions:

## Individual Counseling

Individual counseling is a personal and private interaction between a counselor and a student in which they work together on a problem or topic of interest. A face-to-face, one-to-one meeting with a counselor provides a student maximum privacy in which to freely explore ideas, feelings, and behaviors. School counselors establish trust and build a helping relationship. They respect the privacy of information, always considering actions in terms of the rights, integrity, and welfare of students. Counselors are obligated by law and ethical standards to report and to refer a case when a person's welfare is in jeopardy. It is a counselor's duty to inform an individual of the conditions and limitations under which assistance may be provided.

## Small Group Counseling

Small group counseling involves a counselor working with two or more students together. Group size generally ranges from five to eight members. Group discussions may be relatively unstructured or may be based on structured learning activities. Group members have an opportunity to learn from each other. They can share ideas, give and receive feedback, increase their awareness, gain new knowledge, practice skills, and think about their goals and actions. Group discussions may be problem-centered, where attention is given to particular concerns or problems. Discussions may be growth-centered, where general topics are related to personal and academic development.

## Large Group Guidance

Large group meetings offer the best opportunity to provide guidance to the largest number of students in a school. Counselors first work with students in large groups wherever appropriate because it is the most efficient use of time. Large group work involves cooperative learning methods, in which the larger group is divided into smaller working groups under the supervision of a counselor or teacher. The guidance and counseling curriculum, composed of organized objectives and activities, is delivered by teachers or counselors in classrooms or advisory groups. School counselors and teachers may co-lead some activities. Counselors develop and present special guidance units which give attention to particular developmental issues or areas of concern in their respective schools and they help prepare teachers to deliver part of the guidance and counseling curriculum.

## Consultation

The counselor as a consultant helps people to be more effective in working with others. Consultation helps individuals think through problems and concerns, acquire more knowledge and skill, and become more objective and self-confident. This intervention can take place in individual or group conferences, or through staff-development activities.

## Coordination

Coordination as a counselor intervention is the process of managing various indirect services which benefit students and being a liaison between school and community agencies. It may include organizing special events which involve parents or resource people in the community in guidance projects. It often entails collecting data and disseminating information. Counselors might coordinate a student needs assessment, the interpretation of standardized tests, a child study team, or a guidance related teacher or parent education program.

## THE PREPARATION OF SCHOOL COUNSELORS

School counselors are prepared for their work through the study of interpersonal relationships and behavioral sciences in graduate education courses in accredited colleges and universities. Preparation involves special training in counseling theory and skills related to school settings. Particular attention is given to personality and human development theories and research, including career and life-skills development; learning theories, the nature of change and the helping process; theories and approaches to appraisal, multi-cultural and community awareness; educational environments; curriculum development; professional ethics; and, program planning, management, and evaluation.

Counselors are prepared to use the basic interventions in a school setting, with special emphasis on the study of helping relationships, facilitate skills, brief counseling; group dynamics and group learning activities; family systems; peer helper programs, multi-cultural and cross-cultural helping approaches; and, educational and community resources for special school populations.

School counselors are aware of their own professional competencies and responsibilities within the school setting. They know when and how to refer or involve other professionals. They are accountable for their actions and participate in appropriate studies and research related to their work.

## RESPONSIBILITY TO THE PROFESSION

To assure high quality practice, counselors are committed to continued professional growth and personal development. They are active members of the American Association for Counseling and Development and the American School Counselor Association, as well as state and local professional associations which foster and promote school counseling. They also uphold the ethical and professional standards of these associations.

School counselors meet the state certification standards and abide by the laws in the states where they are working. Counselors work cooperatively with individuals and organizations to promote the overall development of children, youth, and families in their communities.

# School Counselor Competencies

## PERSONAL CHARACTERISTICS OF EFFECTIVE COUNSELORS

The personal attributes or characteristics of school counselors are very important to their success. Effective counselors usually

- have a genuine interest in the welfare of others.
- are able to understand the perspective of others.
- believe individuals are capable of solving problems.
- are open to learning.
- are willing to take risks.
- have a strong sense of self-worth.
- are not afraid of making mistakes and attempt to learn from them.
- value continued growth as a person.
- are caring and warm.
- possess a keen sense of humor.

## SCHOOL COUNSELOR COMPETENCIES

School counselors must know various theories and concepts (knowledge competencies) and must be able to utilize a variety of skills (skill competen-

---

SOURCE: American School Counselor Association. (1990). *School counselor competencies*. Alexandria, VA: Author. Reprinted with permission.

cies). Further, they must be competent professionals and effective persons. The competencies needed by today's counselors are presented below:

## KNOWLEDGE COMPETENCIES

School counselors need to **know**

- human development theories and concepts
- individual counseling theories
- consultation theories and techniques
- family counseling theories and techniques
- group counseling theories and techniques
- career decision-making theories and techniques
- learning theories
- motivation theories
- the effect of culture on individual development and behavior
- evaluation theories and processes
- ethical and legal issues related to counseling
- program development models

## SKILL COMPETENCIES

School counselors should be able to demonstrate **skills** in

- diagnosing student needs
- individual counseling
- group counseling
- consultation with staff, students, and parents
- coordination of programs, e.g., testing, career development, substance abuse
- career counseling
- educational counseling
- identifying and making appropriate referrals
- administering and interpreting achievement, interest, aptitude, and personality tests
- cross-cultural counseling
- ethical decision-making
- building supportive climates for students and staff
- removing and/or decreasing race and gender bias in school policy and curriculum

- explaining to the staff, community, and parents, the scope of practice and functions of a school counselor
- planning and conducting inservice for staff
- identifying resources and information related to helping clients
- evaluating the effectiveness of counseling programs

## PROFESSIONAL COMPETENCIES

School counselors should be able to

- conduct a self-evaluation to determine their strengths and areas needing improvement
- develop a plan of personal and professional growth to enable them to participate in lifelong learning
- advocate for appropriate state and national legislation
- adopt a set of professional ethics to guide their practice and interactions with students, staff, community, parents, and peers

# ASCA Position Statement: The School Counselor and Developmental Guidance

## THE POSITION OF THE AMERICAN SCHOOL COUNSELOR ASSOCIATION (ASCA)

*Developmental guidance should be an integral part of every school counseling program and be incorporated into the role and function of every school counselor.*

## THE RATIONALE

During recent years a number of counselor educators and school counselors have advanced the proposition that counseling can and should be more proactive and preventive in its focus and more developmental in its content and process. Viewed in the context of evolving societal emphasis upon personal growth and an expanding professional expertise, developmental guidance has resulted in a potentially dynamic and promising approach to the helping relationship of the school counselor. Developmental guidance is a reaffirmation and actualization of the belief that guidance is for all students and that its purpose is to maximally facilitate personal development.

There are several general principles which should help insure quality and effectiveness in the implementation of developmental guidance:

1. The program should be systematic, sequential, and comprehensive.
2. The program should be jointly founded upon developmental psychology, educational philosophy, and counseling methodology.

SOURCE: American School Counselor Association. (1984). *Position statement: The school counselor and developmental guidance.* Alexandria, VA: Author. Reprinted with permission.

3. Both process and product (of the program itself and the individuals in it) should be stressed.
4. All the personal domains—cognitive, affective, behavioral, experiential, and environmental—should be emphasized.
5. Programs should emphasize preparation for the future and consolidation of the present.
6. Individualization and transfer learning should be central to program procedure and method.
7. Evaluation and corrective feedback are essential.

APPENDIX **E**

# ASCA Ethical Standards for School Counselors

**PREAMBLE**

The American School Counselor Association (ASCA) is a professional organization whose members have a unique and distinctive preparation, grounded in the behavioral sciences, with training in counseling skills adapted to the school setting. The school counselor assists in the growth and development of each individual and uses his/her specialized skills to ensure that the rights of the counselee are properly protected within the structure of the school program. School counselors subscribe to the following basic tenets of the counseling process from which professional responsibilities are derived:

1. Each person has the right to respect and dignity as a unique human being and to counseling services without prejudice as to person, character, belief or practice.
2. Each person has the right to self-direction and self-development.
3. Each person has the right of choice and the responsibility for decisions reached.
4. Each person has the right to privacy and thereby the right to expect the counselor-client relationship to comply with all laws, policies and ethical standards pertaining to confidentiality.

In this document, the American School Counselor Association has specified the principles of ethical behavior necessary to maintain and regulate the

SOURCE: American School Counselor Association. (1992). *Ethical standards for school counselors.* Revised as approved by the ASCA Delegate Assembly, March 27. Alexandria, VA: Author. Reprinted with permission.

high standards of integrity and leadership among its members. The Association recognizes the basic commitment of its members in the *Ethical Standards* of its parent organization, the American Counseling Association (ACA), and nothing in this document shall be construed to supplant that code. *The Ethical Standards for School Counselors* was developed to complement the ACA standards by clarifying the nature of ethical responsibilities for present and future counselors in the school setting. The purposes of this document are to:

1. Serve as a guide for the ethical practices of all professional school counselors regardless of level, area, population served, or membership in this Association.
2. Provide benchmarks for both self-appraisal and peer evaluations regarding counselor responsibilities to students, parents, colleagues and professional associates, school and community, self, and the counseling profession.
3. Inform those served by the school counselor of acceptable counselor practices and expected professional deportment.

## A. RESPONSIBILITIES TO STUDENTS

The school counselor:

1. Has a primary obligation and loyalty to the student, who is to be treated with respect as a unique individual, whether assisted individually or in a group setting.
2. Is concerned with the total needs of the student (educational, vocational, personal and social) and encourages the maximum growth and development of each counselee.
3. Informs the counselee of the purposes, goals, techniques and rules of procedure under which she/he may receive counseling assistance at or before the time when the counseling relationship is entered. Prior notice includes confidentiality issues such as the possible necessity for consulting with other professionals, privileged communication, and legal or authoritative restraints. The meaning and limits of confidentiality are clearly defined to counselees.
4. Refrains from consciously encouraging the counselee's acceptance of values, lifestyles, plans, decisions, and beliefs that represent only the counselor's personal orientation.
5. Is responsible for keeping abreast of laws relating to students and strives to ensure that the rights of students are adequately provided for and protected.
6. Avoids dual relationships which might impair his/her objectivity and/or increase the risk of harm to the client (e.g., counseling one's family members, close friends or associates). If a dual

relationship is unavoidable, the counselor is responsible for taking action to eliminate or reduce the potential for harm. Such safeguards might include informed consent, consultation, supervision and documentation.

7. Makes appropriate referrals when professional assistance can no longer be adequately provided to the counselee. Appropriate referral requires knowledge of available resources.

8. Protects the confidentiality of student records and releases personal data only according to prescribed laws and school policies. Student information maintained through electronic data storage methods is treated with the same care as traditional student records.

9. Protects the confidentiality of information received in the counseling relationship as specified by law and ethical standards. Such information is only to be revealed to others with the informed consent of the counselee and consistent with the obligations of the counselor as a professional person. In a group setting, the counselor sets a norm of confidentiality and stresses its importance, yet clearly states that confidentiality in group counseling cannot be guaranteed.

10. Informs the appropriate authorities when the counselee's condition indicates a clear and imminent danger to the counselee or others. This is to be done after careful deliberation and, where possible, after consultation with other professionals. The counselor informs the counselee of actions to be taken so as to minimize confusion and clarify expectations.

11. Screens prospective group members and maintains an awareness of participants' compatibility throughout the life of the group, especially when the group emphasis is on self-disclosure and self-understanding. The counselor takes reasonable precautions to protect members from physical and/or psychological harm resulting from interaction within the group.

12. Provides explanations of the nature, purposes, and results of tests in language that is understandable to the client(s).

13. Adheres to relevant standards regarding selection, administration, and interpretation of assessment techniques. The counselor recognizes that computer-based testing programs require specific training in administration, scoring and interpretation which may differ from that required in more traditional assessments.

14. Promotes the benefits of appropriate computer applications and clarifies the limitations of computer technology. The counselor ensures that (1) computer applications are appropriate for the individual needs of the counselee, (2) the counselee understands how to use the application, and (3) follow-up counseling assistance is provided. Members of underrepresented groups are assured of equal access to computer technologies and the absence

of discriminatory information and values within computer applications.

15. Has unique ethical responsibilities in working with peer programs. In general, the school counselor is responsible for the welfare of students participating in peer programs under his/her direction. School counselors who function in training and supervisory capacities are referred to the preparation and supervision standards of professional counselor associations.

## B. RESPONSIBILITIES TO PARENTS

The school counselor:

1. Respects the inherent rights and responsibilities of parents for their children and endeavors to establish a cooperative relationship with parents to facilitate the maximum development of the counselee.
2. Informs parents of the counselor's role, with emphasis on the confidential nature of the counseling relationship between the counselor and counselee.
3. Provides parents with accurate, comprehensive and relevant information in an objective and caring manner, as appropriate and consistent with ethical responsibilities to the counselee.
4. Treats information received from parents in a confidential and appropriate manner.
5. Shares information about a counselee only with those persons properly authorized to receive such information.
6. Adheres to laws and local guidelines when assisting parents experiencing family difficulties which interfere with the counselee's effectiveness and welfare.
7. Is sensitive to changes in the family and recognizes that all parents, custodial and noncustodial, are vested with certain rights and responsibilities for the welfare of their children by virtue of their position and according to law.

## C. RESPONSIBILITIES TO COLLEAGUES AND PROFESSIONAL ASSOCIATES

The school counselor:

1. Establishes and maintains a cooperative relationship with faculty, staff and administration to facilitate the provision of optimal guidance and counseling programs and services.
2. Promotes awareness and adherence to appropriate guidelines regarding confidentiality, the distinction between public and private information, and staff consultation.

3. Treats colleagues with respect, courtesy, fairness and good faith. The qualifications, views and findings of colleagues are represented accurately and fairly to enhance the image of competent professionals.
4. Provides professional personnel with accurate, objective, concise and meaningful data necessary to adequately evaluate, counsel and assist the counselee.
5. Is aware of and fully utilizes related professions and organizations to whom the counselee may be referred.

## D. RESPONSIBILITIES TO THE SCHOOL AND COMMUNITY

The school counselor:

1. Supports and protects the educational program against any infringement not in the best interest of students.
2. Informs appropriate officials of conditions that may be potentially disruptive or damaging to the school's mission, personnel and property.
3. Delineates and promotes the counselor's role and function in meeting the needs of those served. The counselor will notify appropriate school officials of conditions which may limit or curtail their effectiveness in providing programs and services.
4. Assists in the development of: (1) curricular and environmental conditions appropriate for the school and community, (2) educational procedures and programs to meet student needs, and (3) a systematic evaluation process for guidance and counseling programs, services and personnel. The counselor is guided by the findings of the evaluation data in planning programs and services.
5. Actively cooperates and collaborates with agencies, organizations, and individuals in the school and community in the best interest of counselees and without regard to personal reward or remuneration.

## E. RESPONSIBILITIES TO SELF

The school counselor:

1. Functions within the boundaries of individual professional competence and accepts responsibility for the consequences of his/her actions.
2. Is aware of the potential effects of her/his own personal characteristics on services to clients.
3. Monitors personal functioning and effectiveness and refrains from any activity likely to lead to inadequate professional services or harm to a client.

4. Recognizes that differences in clients relating to age, gender, race, religion, sexual orientation, socioeconomic and ethnic backgrounds may require specific training to ensure competent services.
5. Strives through personal initiative to maintain professional competence and keep abreast of innovations and trends in the profession. Professional and personal growth is continuous and ongoing throughout the counselor's career.

## F. RESPONSIBILITIES TO THE PROFESSION

The school counselor:

1. Conducts herself/himself in such a manner as to bring credit to self and the profession.
2. Conducts appropriate research and reports findings in a manner consistent with acceptable educational and psychological research practices. When using client data for research, statistical or program planning purposes, the counselor ensures protection of the identity of the individual client(s).
3. Actively participates in local, state and national associations which foster the development and improvement of school counseling.
4. Adheres to ethical standards of the profession, other official policy statements pertaining to counseling, and relevant statutes established by federal, state and local governments.
5. Clearly distinguishes between statements and actions made as a private individual and as a representative of the school counseling profession.
6. Contributes to the development of the profession through the sharing of skills, ideas and expertise with colleagues.

## G. MAINTENANCE OF STANDARDS

Ethical behavior among professional school counselors, Association members and nonmembers, is expected at all times. When there exists serious doubt as to the ethical behavior of colleagues, or if counselors are forced to work in situations or abide by policies which do not reflect the standards as outlined in these *Ethical Standards for School Counselors* or the ACA *Ethical Standards*, the counselor is obligated to take appropriate action to rectify the condition. The following procedure may serve as a guide:

1. If feasible, the counselor should consult with a professional colleague to confidentially discuss the nature of the complaint to see if she/he views the situation as an ethical violation.
2. Whenever possible, the counselor should directly approach the colleague whose behavior is in question to discuss the complaint and seek resolution.

3. If resolution is not forthcoming at the personal level, the counselor shall utilize the channels established within the school and/or school district. This may include both informal and formal procedures.
4. If the matter still remains unresolved, referral for review and appropriate action should be made to the Ethics Committees in the following sequence:
   - local counselor association
   - state counselor association
   - national counselor association
5. The ASCA Ethics Committee functions in an educative and consultative capacity and does not adjudicate complaints of ethical misconduct. Therefore, at the national level, complaints should be submitted in writing to the ACA Ethics Committee for review and appropriate action. The procedure for submitting complaints may be obtained by writing the ACA Ethics Committee, c/o The Executive Director, American Counseling Association, 5999 Stevenson Avenue, Alexandria, VA 22304.

## H. RESOURCES

School counselors are responsible for being aware of, and acting in accord with, the standards and positions of the counseling profession as represented in official documents such as those listed below.

*Code of Ethics* (1989). National Board for Certified Counselors. Alexandria, VA.

*Code of Ethics for Peer Helping Professionals* (1989). National Peer Helpers Association. Glendale, CA.

*Ethical Guidelines for Group Counselors* (1989). Association for Specialists in Group Work. Alexandria, VA.

*Ethical Standards* (1988). American Association for Counseling and Development. Alexandria, VA.

*Position Statement: The School Counselor and Confidentiality* (1986). American School Counselor Association. Alexandria, VA.

*Position Statement: The School Counselor and Peer Facilitation* (1984). American School Counselor Association. Alexandria, VA.

*Position Statement: The School Counselor and Student Rights* (1982). American School Counselor Association. Alexandria, VA.

# References

American Psychology Association. (1956). Division of Counseling Psychology. Committee on Definition. Washington, DC: Author.

Borders, D. L., & Drury, S. M. (1992). Comprehensive school counseling programs. *Journal of Counseling and Development, 70,* 487–498.

Carr, J. V., Hayslip, J. B., & Randall, J. (1988). *New Hampshire comprehensive guidance and counseling program: A model for program development.* Plymouth, NH: Plymouth State College.

Cattell, R. B., & Institute Staff. (1991). *16 PF© Sixteen personality factor questionnaire.* Champaign, IL: Institute for Personality and Ability Testing.

Drier, H., Jones, B., & Jones, L. (1985). *Legislative provisions for the development of comprehensive community-based career guidance programs.* Wooster, OH: Bell and Howell.

Durgin, R., & Drier, H. (1991). *How to fund career guidance programs.* Omro, WI: Coordinated Occupational Information Network.

Dye, H. A., & Borders, L. D. (1990). Counseling supervisor: Standards for preparation and practice. *Journal of Counseling and Development, 69,* 27–29.

Gilkey, J. K., & Berg, I. K. (1991). *A school interview in two parts: The solution-based model.* Milwaukee, WI: Brief Family Therapy Center.

Gysbers, N. C., & Henderson, P. (1988). *Developing and managing your school guidance program.* Alexandria, VA: American Association for Counseling and Development.

Gysbers, N. C., Hughey, K. F. Starr, M., & Lapan, R. T. (1992). Improving school guidance programs: A framework for program, personnel, and results evaluation. *Journal of Counseling and Development, 70,* 565–570.

Hall, M. (1988). *Getting funded: A complete guide to proposal writing.* Portland, OR: Continuing Education Publications.

Hersey, P., & Blanchard, K. H. (1992). *Leadership effectiveness and adaptability description (LEAD).* Escondido, CA: Leadership Studies.

Johnson, S. K., & Whitfield, E. A. (1991). *Evaluating guidance programs: A practi-*

*tioner's guide*. Iowa City, IA: American College Testing and the National Consortium of State Career Guidance Supervisors.

National Occupational Information Coordinating Committee. (1989). *National career development guidelines*. Washington, DC: Author.

McCharen, B. (1990). *Self-assessment of counselor inservice training needs*. Stillwater: Oklahoma Department of Vocational and Technical Education.

Myers, I. B., & Briggs, K. (1992). *Myers-Briggs type indicator*. Palo Alto, CA: Counseling Psychologists Press.

Myrick, R. D. (1993). *Developmental guidance and counseling*. Minneapolis, MN: Educational Media.

Painter, L., & VanZandt, C. E. (1988). Unpublished assessment. Gorham: University of Southern Maine.

Pfieffer, J. W., & Jones, J. E. (Eds.). (1976). Role functions in a group. In *The 1976 Annual Handbook for Group Facilitators*. San Diego, CA: Pfieffer and Company.

Piaget, J. (1969). *The mechanisms of perception*. (G. N. Seagrim, trans.). New York: Basic Books.

Supervision Interest Network, Association for Counselor Education and Supervision. (1990). *Standards for Counseling Supervisors*. Alexandria, VA: American Association for Counseling and Development.

VanZandt, C. E. (1990). Professionalism: A matter of personal initiative. *Journal of Counseling and Development, 68*, 243–245.

Wysong, E. (1973). Accountability: Foibled fable or solution. *Impact, 2*, 34–37.

# Index

## Text Evaluation Form for Course Instructors

1. What did you find most useful about *Your Comprehensive School Guidance and Counseling Program*? Least?

_____

_____

_____

_____

_____

_____

_____

_____

_____

_____

_____

_____

2. What changes or additions should be made for the next edition?

_____

_____

_____

_____

_____

_____

_____

_____

_____

_____

3. Please add comments that you believe would be helpful.

_____

_____

_____

_____

_____

_____

_____

_____

_____

_____

Please return to either C.E. VanZandt, 400 Bailey Hall, University of Southern Maine, Gorham, ME 04038, or J.B. Hayslip, Memorial 110, Plymouth State College, Plymouth, NH 03264.